Old-Time Fiddle

Round Peak Style

CD Included With 83 Tunes

History, Tips, & Techniques

BY Brad Leftwich

Cover designed by Steve Millard • Cover photo of Brad © 2007 R.L. Geyer

CD contents

1 Baby-o	25 Police	45 Ducks on the Mill Pond	66 Susananna Gal
2 Big-Eyed Rabbit	26 Poor Ellen Smith	46 Fall on My Knees	(Western Country)
3 The Blackest Crow	27 Pretty Little Girl	47 Fisher's Hornpipe	67 Tempie
(My Dearest Sweetheart)	28 Pretty Polly	48 Forky Deer	68 They Say It Is Sinful to Flirt
4 Breaking up Christmas	29 Rainbow Sign	49 Fortune	(Willie My Darling)
5 Chilly Winds	30 Round Town Gals	50 The Joke on the Puppy	69 The Wreck of the Old 97
6 Cluck Old Hen	(Buffalo Gals)	(Rye Straw)	70 The Yellow Rose of Texas
7 Cotton-Eyed Joe	31 Ruben	51 Mississippi Sawyer	71 Boll Weevil
8 Cripple Creek	32 Shortening Bread	52 New River Train	72 Bonaparte's Retreat
9 Darling Nellie Grey	33 Sourwood Mountain	53 Old Jimmy Sutton	73 Ryland Spencer
10 Fire on the Mountain	34 Stay All Night	54 Old Molly Hare	74 Frankie Baker
11 Granny, Will Your Dog Bite?	35 Sweet Sunny South	55 Peek-a-Boo (Green Gravel)	(Frankie and Albert)
12 Greasy String	36 The Tater Patch Tune	56 Polly Put the Kettle On	75 Tumblin Gap
13 Groundhog	37 Train on the Island	57 Richmond Cotillion	(Cumberland Gap)
14 Ida Red	38 When Sorrows	58 Ricketts' Hornpipe	76 Flatwoods
15 John Brown's Dream	Encompass Me Round	59 Rochester Schottische	77 Cackling Hen
16 John Hardy	39 The Drunken Hiccups	(Walking in the Parlor)	78 Dance All Night
17 John Henry	(Jack of Diamonds)	60 Rockingham Cindy	with a Bottle in Your Hand
18 June Apple	40 Arkansas Traveler	61 Sally Ann	79 Devil in the Strawstack
19 Kitty Clyde (Katy Cline)	41 Backstep Cindy	62 "Old-Time" Sally Ann	80 Old Buck
20 Let Me Fall (Old Hard Road)	(Stepback Cindy)	63 Say, Darling, Say	(Paddy on the Turnpike)
21 Little Maggie	42 "Old-Time" Backstep Cindy	64 Soldier's Joy	81 Piney Woods Gal
22 Lonesome Road Blues	(Holly Ding)	(Love Somebody)	82 Sail Away Ladies
23 Old Bunch of Keys	43 The Bravest Cowboy	65 Sugar Hill	83 Walking in My Sleep
24 Old Joe Clark	44 Cider (Stillhouse)		

D1597806

Visit us on the Web at www.melbay.com — E-mail us at email@melbay.com

Contents

List of tunes (alphabetical by tuning)

Preface

"Ain't no use, if a fellow can't handle a bow, he'll never make no fiddler. He might make a violinist—but he can't make no fiddler."

—Tommy Jarrell, traditional Round Peak fiddler

Learning from Tommy Jarrell

In the old days, aspiring fiddlers grew up immersed in the music of their own communities and learned it as naturally as they learned to speak. In modern times, however, many people who are attracted to old-time fiddling don't have that opportunity, and without early immersion, discovering how to get a truly traditional sound can be a challenge akin to becoming fluent in a second language. I went through that process trying to reclaim my family's musical legacy, and this book is part of my efforts to share what I discovered.

Brad and Tommy, 1982

I grew up in Oklahoma in the 1950s and have warm memories of visiting my grandparents' farm in Kansas. I heard the old-time banjo and fiddle duets of my grandfather and his brother, Rush and George Leftwich, who migrated from near Fancy Gap in Virginia's Blue Ridge Mountains early in the century. Both passed away around the time I was ten years old, but the sound of their music made a lasting impression on me. That was the sound I wanted to emulate when I took up the banjo and fiddle as a teenager. For a couple of years I picked up what I could, wherever I could; but I didn't have much to go on until, in 1973, I had the good fortune to meet Tommy Jarrell.

Tommy was originally from Round Peak, a community in Surry County, North Carolina, no more than a dozen miles from where my grandfather was raised. I was 20 when we met; Tommy was 72. He was already a celebrity in the small but growing world of old-time music enthusiasts, a master fiddler and banjo player whose duets with Fred Cockerham expressed the epitome of pre-commercial mountain music.

Not only was Tommy a charismatic personality and a great musician, it turned out we had a family connection: his mother-in-law, Ardena Leftwich, was my grandfather's cousin. Tommy was just a child when Rush moved to Kansas, but he knew of him and in fact had played music with Ken and Amelia Leftwich, Rush's brother and sister who remained behind. Needless to say, I was hooked. Although I learned from other traditional fiddlers as well, Tommy remained my mentor and friend until his death in 1985.

Making a fiddler

As inspirational as Tommy was, just visiting and playing with him was no guarantee of learning what he had to teach. You really had to heed his advice to watch his bow arm, which, in his opinion, "does all the work." And if the lesson was lost even on many visitors who watched him play and heard his admonitions about bowing, you can imagine the odds faced by those trying to figure it out on their own.

So in the 20-plus years I've been teaching others to fiddle, I have focused largely on bowing, and I believe it's the most important contribution of this book. These are examples of how the tunes would actually be played by a traditional fiddler—not just abstract melodies with the bowing and other critical matters of style left to the imagination. Many of the tunes are well known precisely because they are great vehicles for the techniques that make old-time fiddling so infectious. Their power is not only in their melodies, as you will come to see.

This is not a starting-from-scratch instructional book, but rather an introduction to style and repertoire for those who already have some facility on the instrument. If you're interested in being an old-time *fiddler*, rather than someone who, in Tommy's words, "knows a thousand tunes but can't play a-one of 'em," then this book is for you. Since many of the fiddle techniques used in the Round Peak area were also widespread throughout the South and wherever Southern musicians migrated, this book makes a good introduction to old-time style in general. None of the tunes are dumbed down, but the natural range of difficulty is such that everyone from beginning-intermediate players to those with mastery of the instrument will find appropriate material.

The book can stand alone as a manual on old-time fiddling, or as a companion to my Mel Bay book, *Round Peak Style Clawhammer Banjo*. Together they provide an inside look at an exciting, intricate fiddle-banjo style that developed in the fertile hotbed of old-time music along the North Carolina–Virginia border. No matter how you came to be interested in old-time music, if you want that real old-time sound, this is a great place to start. The Round Peak tradition is subtle, rich, and a lot of fun to play.

Acknowledgements

Linda Higginbotham, my wife and longtime musical partner, should be listed as co-author of this book, but she preferred not to be named on the cover. I am more grateful than I can ever adequately express for her help with this book as well as for our shared life of music from which it has grown. My gratitude also to my father, Dick Leftwich, whose singing and guitar playing were the first old-time music I ever heard, and who has always enthusiastically supported my musical interests. A special tip-of-the-hat to artist Steve Millard for designing the cover and creating the delightful map on page 6; to photographer R. L. Geyer for the picture of me on the cover; to Jon Anderson for helping me get started making the recordings and for carefully reading the manuscript; and to Cathy Fink for offering good recording advice and lending her keen ears to a sample of the results.

I'm indebted to the people listed below who had the foresight and energy to preserve a wealth of information about Round Peak music and the generosity to allow me to use it in this book. Without their labors of love, much of that lore would by now have vanished with the passing of the older generation. To supplement the stories Tommy Jarrell told me in person, I've drawn extensively on their work (see "Recommended listening, viewing, and reading," p. 124) in writing profiles of musicians and introductions to tunes.

First and foremost I'd like to thank Kevin Donleavy, who spent years tracking down and interviewing musicians and their families, uncovering old photos, and locating birthplaces and final resting places. The results are published in his book, *Strings of Life—Conversations with Old-Time Musicians from Virginia and North Carolina*. It's a gold mine of oral history and information about genealogy, geography, personalities, and the complicated web of relationships among musicians in Round Peak and surrounding areas.

Special thanks also to the late Ray Alden, who was involved with Round Peak music since the 1960s. He made countless field recordings and wrote articles, liner notes, and personal communications that have proven extremely useful to me in this project. He was a tireless promoter of the music and a true friend to the entire community. Among his legacies is the Field Recorders' Collective label, one of the most important sources of non-commercial recordings of traditional music. The label's profits are plowed back into making this music available to fans and benefiting the families of musicians.

Thanks to Nancy Dols Neithammer, who gave me permission to draw on transcripts of Tommy Jarrell's family stories that she published in a pair of articles for *The Old-Time Herald*, and to Barry Poss, Richard Nevins, and the late Mike Seeger for record liner notes that were full of useful information. I'm grateful to Wayne Erbsen for letting me quote from his recordings of conversations with Tommy during a visit he and Andy Cahan made in 1980, accessible online through the Digital Library of Appalachia.

Others who have generously responded to my requests for help and information include Alice Gerrard, Kerry Blech, and Paul Brown. Thanks also to Kevin Donleavy, Ray Alden, Cece Conway, David Lynch, Kirk Sutphin, Philip DeLoach, and Reavis Lyons for their help in rounding up photos for this book.

This entire book attests to the enormous debt I owe Tommy Jarrell for his hospitality and boundless generosity with his music and time. I'd also like to express my thanks to his late sons B.F. and Wayne for their longtime friendship, and in particular to his daughter Ardena Moncus who, over the years since Tommy's death, has treated Linda and me like family and extended the same Jarrell hospitality that her father did.

Round Peak: a hill, a community, a tradition

Round Peak in context

To old-time music fans around the world, the name "Round Peak" is legendary, bringing to mind the exhilarating, intricate fiddle-banjo duets of Tommy Jarrell and Fred Cockerham, and the tight, hard-driving band sound of the Camp Creek Boys and its offshoots. Because Round Peak is so often invoked at jam sessions, festivals, and in Internet discussions, people often suppose that it encompasses a broad area of the southern Appalachians. But in fact it properly refers only to one small community in Surry County, N.C., that, thanks to its highly developed music and the number of excellent musicians it produced, has had a disproportionate influence on the modern old-time music scene.

The community takes its name from a hill at the foot of Fisher's Peak, which marks the point where the Blue Ridge Mountains cross the North Carolina–Virginia state line. Other communities known for their music are nearby, notably Galax, Va., which lies some 15 miles away on the other side of the ridge.

Despite the proximity of the two communities, "Round Peak" and "Galax" aren't interchangeable stylistic labels. To Round Peakers, Galax was "the backside of the mountain." Nowadays good roads and modern communication have blurred the musical distinctions among them, but back when most travel was on foot or horseback along dirt roads, 15 miles was a long distance to go and the Blue Ridge was an imposing barrier. Musicians got around, of course, and elements of style and repertoire were widely shared, but the musical identities of Round Peak and Galax were distinct enough that musicians on both sides of the ridge remarked on it.

By contrast, there was much more visiting and sharing among musicians from communities along the foot and southeast slope of the ridge, from Low Gap to Round Peak in Surry County, N.C., on up to Lambsburg and Pipers Gap in Carroll County, Va. Tommy Jarrell had occasion to associate with musicians as far away as Fancy Gap, also in Carroll County and still within about 10 miles of his home.

Round Peak fiddling, old and new

Due to limitations of time and space, this book focuses on the old-style fiddling from just after the turn of the twentieth century, exemplified by the playing of Tommy Jarrell. Born in 1901, Tommy was at the tail end of the pre-commercial era. The explosion of the radio and recording industries during the 1920s and '30s revolutionized the nation's musical landscape, and Round Peak was no exception to the trend. New instruments like the guitar, mandolin, and bass began to augment the traditional banjo-fiddle duet, and the jazzy fiddling of Arthur Smith, broadcast on WSM's Grand Ole Opry radio program out of Nashville, was particularly influential among aspiring fiddlers just a few years younger than Tommy—even among some his own age.

The result of this great musical watershed is that Round Peak fiddling encompasses both an older style that we know mostly through Tommy's music, and a newer style showcased by fiddlers in the region's big string bands. Anyone interested in learning more about the differences between the two should have a look at Barry Poss' notes to *The Legacy of Tommy Jarrell, vol. 1: Sail Away Ladies* (County CD-2724).

Tommy began fiddling about 1914, and his style and repertoire, learned mostly from older family members and neighbors in a traditional community setting, were pretty well established by the early 1920s. Tommy's extensive use of drone strings in specialized tunings, subtle ornamentation, and complex bowing rhythms hark back to the late nineteenth century, when a dance band was at most a fiddle and a banjo. A few recordings exist of Tommy's father, Ben Jarrell—enough to show the striking similarity of their playing—but other than those, Tommy's recordings are the best representation we have of the older Round Peak fiddle style, and we're fortunate that he was extensively documented before his death in 1985.

I had hoped to include a section on the music of Round Peak fiddlers who came later. Most of my experience, however, is with Tommy's music, and in fact it turned out that his repertoire alone gave me more than enough material for a book. I hope that someone better acquainted with the newer style will follow up my efforts and round out our picture of the music of this remarkable area.

The area around the turn of the 20th century

Tommy's tunes and stories open a window onto a fascinating musical scene that flourished a century ago, a time when there was no entertainment but what people made themselves. Most of his tunes came from his father and uncle, but he also learned from neighbors in Surry County as well as musicians across the state line in Carroll County, Va. The area in which he learned most of his music stretches for about 15 miles along the Blue Ridge, from Low Gap, N.C., to Fancy Gap, Va.

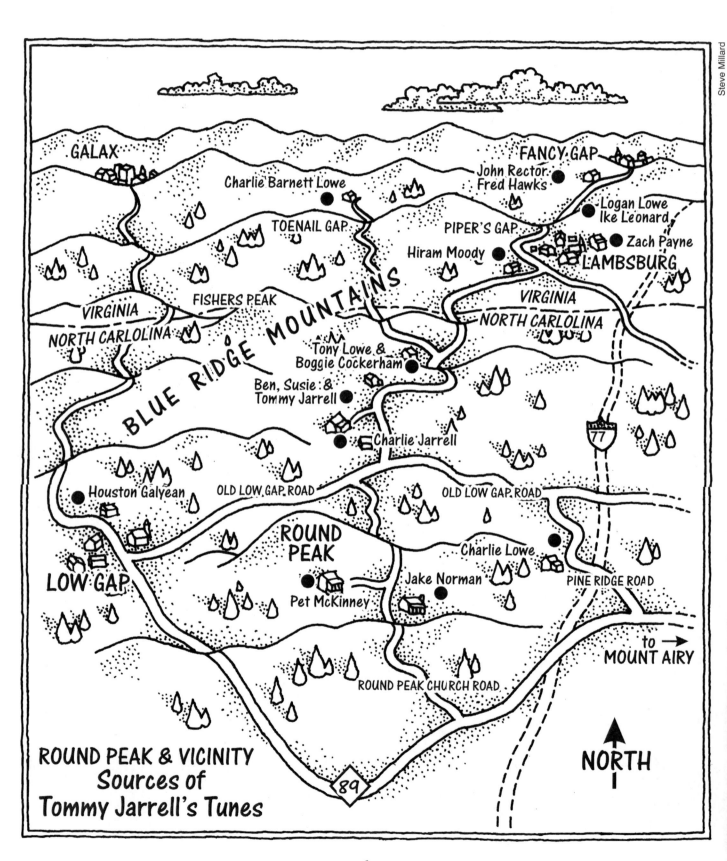

ROUND PEAK & VICINITY
Sources of
Tommy Jarrell's Tunes

Steve Millard

Tommy Jarrell and the fiddlers who influenced him

Below are brief profiles of Tommy and some of the fiddlers he credited as sources for his tunes. Profiles of other influential musicians are interspersed among the transcriptions.

Tommy Jarrell (1901–1985)

Tommy was born into a large, musical family. His grandmother, father, uncle, and many of his brothers and sisters were musicians. Tommy began making music when he was seven or eight years old, playing banjo behind the fiddling of his father, Ben Jarrell. He took up fiddle himself at age 13. Tommy paid close attention to the fiddling of his father and uncle Charlie Jarrell in particular, and took advantage of any opportunity to learn from other fiddlers as well.

Earning a living in the mountains was difficult. Tommy tried farming as a young man, but discovered he could do better making liquor. About 1920, in the aftermath of a serious fight with his uncle, Tommy spent some time just over the Virginia state line, working for and boarding at the home of family friend and banjo picker Charlie Barnett Lowe (not to be confused with Charlie Lowe, the legendary banjo picker from Round Peak). Tommy learned a number of tunes from Charlie Barnett and other musicians in Carroll County, and married Charlie's daughter Nina in 1923. Tommy and Nina moved to Mount Airy, and Tommy drove a motor grader for the North Carolina highway department from 1925 until his retirement in 1966.

Banjo picker Charlie Lowe of Round Peak (see p. 26) was Tommy's main musical partner from about 1916 until Charlie's death in 1964. A few home recordings attest to

Tommy Jarrell, 1982

the skill and intensity of their fiddle-banjo duets. Although Tommy continued to play some during the years he was working and raising a family, his musical career really blossomed after retirement when his fiddling became known worldwide through recordings and concert appearances. Tommy welcomed anyone and everyone into his home, encouraging younger musicians who wanted to learn his music.

Ben Jarrell (1880–1946)

The son of Rufus and Susan Turney Jarrell, Tommy's father was a prominent musician and citizen of the Round Peak community. He was the Round Peak postman from 1914 until 1918 and once ran for public office. He traveled out West for a couple of years, spending some time in an Oregon jail for making whiskey. He returned home in 1920, moved to Toast, N.C., on the outskirts of Mount Airy, and settled down as a storekeeper.

Especially noted as a fiddler, Ben also played banjo. His daughter Julie Lyons said that he and his brother Charlie got their music from their mother, who sang and played fiddle and banjo. Ben's reputation as a musician led Galax entrepreneur DaCosta Woltz to ask him to join the Southern Broadcasters, a band he put together as a commercial venture in 1927. Although not financially successful, the recordings were of immeasurable value in preserving some of Ben's fiddling and singing for posterity.

Ben Jarrell, 1901

Charlie Jarrell (1874–1943)

Tommy's uncle was a colorful character. He and his brother Ben Jarrell got started in music listening to the banjo and fiddle playing of their mother. Like Tommy, Charlie was a moonshiner. He sometimes learned tunes on his travels, such as "Police" and "John Henry," and introduced them into the local repertoire. Round Peak musician Paul Sutphin thought Charlie was a better fiddler than Ben. His regular playing partner Cyrus Lawson remembered that he liked his music very fast.

Charlie Jarrell, 1901

Charlie's daughter Ella said of her father, "He was easy going. My daddy was a good person. When he'd get to drinking, he'd talk a lot. And he wouldn't be run over; didn't nobody ever whip Daddy." Others agreed with Tommy's assessment: "Uncle Charlie, well, he was a good fellow when he was sober, but he was mean as the devil when he was drinking." And then, according to Paul Sutphin, "he was liable to do anything."

After the storied fight with Tommy in 1920, Charlie took out warrants for the arrest of his nephew, who hopped across the nearby state line and waited for the storm to blow over. Neither one seemed to bear hard feelings over the incident: "I reckon it all worked out for the best," Tommy said. No recordings of Charlie's fiddling are known to exist, but Tommy could mimic it well and on certain tunes would often make the last go-round an imitation of his uncle's distinctive sound. "He jerked his bow different than I do," he'd say.

Tony Lowe (1883–1914)

Tona Hawks—his given name at birth—was raised just to the north of the Jarrells in the musical household of his grandfather, banjo picker Kenny Lowe, and came to be known as Tony Lowe. (Bauga "Boggie" Cockerham, who taught Tommy Jarrell his first banjo tune, was raised in the same household.) Tony is remembered as one of the preeminent local fiddlers, a regular playing partner of Round Peak legends Ben Jarrell and Charlie Lowe. He shares credit for the souped-up "Sally Ann" and "Backstep Cindy" that have come to epitomize the Round Peak sound and all but eclipsed the older versions of those tunes in the area. Lambsburg fiddler Hiram Moody was among his admirers, calling Tony the best old-time fiddler he ever heard play. Said Tommy Jarrell: "There's a lot of folks say he could out-fiddle my daddy. But a lot of folks would rather hear my daddy play because he'd sing with his playing." Tony died at age 31 when typhoid fever swept the area. His widow sold his fiddle to Ben Jarrell, and young Tommy learned his first few tunes on it before getting a fiddle of his own.

Pet McKinney with unidentified women

Pet McKinney (1846–1926)

William Preston McKinney, or "Pet" as he was called, was probably the oldest fiddler in the Round Peak area when Tommy was growing up. He was a member of the 45th Virginia Regiment during the Civil War and was a friend and contemporary of Tommy's grandfather, Rufus Jarrell—himself a Confederate veteran. Pet would have been about 70 years old when Tommy, on his way to play for a dance as a teenager, met him in the road. Tommy described learning Pet's unusual and darkly beautiful "Sail Away Ladies" right on the spot. Paul Sutphin credited him as the local source for "Breaking up Christmas." Tommy's "Joke on the Puppy" also came from Pet by way of Ben Jarrell, and it's likely that a couple of other tunes Tommy learned from his dad came originally from him as well. Pet and his wife died within an hour's time of each other.

Houston Galyean (1853–c1906)

Houston Galyean lived near Low Gap, N.C. His brother Toliver was also a fiddler, and Toliver's son Friel often played banjo with Houston. His daughter Eva married the noted banjo and fiddle player Fred Cockerham. Houston is especially remembered for playing "The Drunken Hiccups," which both Ben and Charlie Jarrell learned from him. Tommy in turn learned the tune from Ben. Often when Tommy played it, he'd tell the story of how Houston died. As he related in *Sprout Wings and Fly,* "Charlie Smith run over old man Houston with a load of tanbark on a wagon and killed him. He was a-layin' in the [old Low Gap] road up yonder. Well, he was pretty bad to drink, I guess he just took a notion he'd lay down and go to sleep. They wasn't no traffic on the roads in them days, you know. Wasn't no cars, just a wagon now and then. Charlie, he started to Mount Airy with a load of tanbark and a yoke of steers, and they just walked right on over him. If he'd had horses or mules, one, they wouldn't have done that. But they just stepped right on over him and the wagon run over him."

Friel and Houston Galyean

Logan and Morgan Lowe mugging for the camera

Logan Lowe (1867–1944)

Another of the Carroll County fiddlers Tommy often visited was Logan Lowe. Nicknamed "Log" (rhymes with "rogue"), he was the brother of Tommy's father-in-law, Charlie Barnett Lowe. People remember him as a natural comedian, "a funny old dude," and tell stories of his playful humor. There were frequent dances at the Logan Lowe household, and Tommy remembered learning "Bonaparte's Retreat" from him at one such event. Log married the widow of his neighbor Ike Leonard, a banjo picker who was the source of the "Tater Patch" tune. Both Logan and Charlie Barnett played music regularly with Fancy Gap fiddler John Rector.

Tommy teased Log and another Lowe brother by using their names in a verse to "Susananna Gal": "Gonna hitch old Logan in the lead, and Morgan in behind / I'm goin' down that rocky road, gonna see that gal of mine."

John Rector (1899–1994) and Fred Hawks (1891–1979)

Two of Logan and Charlie Barnett Lowe's regular music partners were fiddlers John Rector and Fred Hawks, both from near Fancy Gap in Carroll County. Tommy sometimes accompanied Charlie Barnett on visits to play music with them and learned several tunes, including "Old Bunch of Keys" and "Forky Deer," from hearing the three of them play. Kevin Donleavy quotes Tommy: "I learned more from him [Charlie] than I did from them; they were both good fiddlers. But John could handle his bow a little better than Fred could." John's prowess as a fiddler was preserved for posterity by the Library of Congress, which made recordings of his band, the Wildcats, in 1937. He won the Galax fiddle contest in 1939, 1941, 1942, and 1945, and continued playing on up to his death in 1994.

John Rector at age 90

9

Hiram Moody, aka Hiram Harris (1888–1966)

The son of fiddler and Confederate veteran Alex Moody, Hiram was the next most prominent fiddler in Lambsburg, Va., after Zach Payne. It's not clear why some knew him as Moody and some as Harris. His son Aldon's description says as much about Lambsburg as it does about Hiram: "My daddy was six foot four inches tall and weighed 240 pounds. Just raw-boned. He carried a .32 special on his hip just as regular as he wore his britches... They wore 'em like that. They didn't believe in taking troubles to the law." Hiram was known to play music with Tony Lowe, Ben Jarrell, and Charlie Lowe. Hiram especially admired and emulated Tony's fiddling, and Charlie Lowe said they sounded very much alike. John Rector said, "He got hold of my fiddle one time, and I thought he was going to tear it up! Playing for a dance at the top of the mountain. He was a good fiddler!" John remembered in particular how Hiram played "Sally Ann," and Tommy Jarrell gave Hiram credit as the source for his low part on that tune.

Courtesy Aldon Harris

Hiram and Alex Moody

Cecelia Conway

Zach Payne's fiddle and headstone

Zach Payne (1845–1929)

Zachariah Payne lived near Lambsburg in Carroll County, not far from the home of Tommy Jarrell's sister Julie. He was a fiddler of legendary stature in his area, and had been a fifer in the Confederate army. Like Pet McKinney, he was a friend of fellow veteran Rufe Jarrell, Tommy's grandfather. Zach was a large man, over 6 feet tall and weighing at least 200 pounds, with long curly hair and a mustache, who enjoyed smoking a corncob pipe. His fiddle, which he carried with him through the war, was much used and abused: It was patched where a rifle ball had struck it; sheet copper covered the worn fingerboard, which was held up off the top by a splinter of pine; and the tailpiece was carved from a cow bone. Visitors found him reluctant to play and had to do a lot of coaxing to hear a tune.

John Rector, who visited him about 1915, said "he was the best fiddler I ever heard." Tommy Jarrell, staying with sister Julie during his Virginia exile in 1920, heard so much about Zach that he went to visit him. Tommy intended to learn "Billy in the Lowground" and "Leather Britches," but instead came away with two more unusual tunes, "Devil in the Strawstack" and "Flatwoods." Tommy agreed with John, to a point: "He was the best fiddler I ever heard—on his tunes, now. 'Course, now, he couldn't play my tunes because he was an old fiddler, you know. I never heard him try "Sally Ann" nor nothing like that." One of Zach's old tunes was "Bonaparte's Retreat"; Logan Lowe learned it from him, and Tommy in turn learned it from Logan.

Using the CD and the book

Listen first!

To get the right sound, it's best to begin by listening, not reading. Old-time fiddling is an aural tradition: in the old days you'd have watched and listened to experienced musicians in your family or community for years before you picked up an instrument. By then you'd know what it should sound like, and from watching you'd have a good idea how to get that sound. Times and technology have changed, but the essential process hasn't.

That's why the CD included with this book is as important as the transcriptions, if not more so: listening to a tune carefully and repeatedly, with all its nuances, is the only way to internalize the sound you're aiming for. You should be able to hear it in your head before you ever pick up your fiddle.

Then look at the transcriptions

Once the sound is in your head, the challenge is to recreate it in your fiddling. Written music can't capture the subtleties of tone, timing, and energy that characterize old-time fiddling, but it can clarify elements like bowing that are hard to hear in a recording. So after you're done listening, start translating what you hear in your head onto your fiddle. When you get stuck, use the transcriptions to help. In this book you'll find two kinds of transcriptions: standard notation and tablature. They align so the information in each can supplement the other.

Standard music notation: The music in the upper staff shows the actual pitch of each note. Keep in mind, however, that most of the tunes are in alternate tunings. It is important to use these tunings, and they change the conventional association between the printed notes and the fingering on any string that's been retuned. The tablature in the lower staff shows the fingering used to get the correct pitches.

Tablature ("tab"): The lower staff uses an easy-to-read system that displays graphically what string to play and which finger to use to get a particular note. The stems that indicate note duration are in the music notation in the upper staff. The exact pitch of a note (whether it's natural or sharp for example) can be ambiguous in the tablature, so when in doubt check the music notation—or better yet, play the CD and use your ears.

Pay close attention to the bowing

More than anything else, syncopated, rhythmically complex bowing (which I believe represents a strong African-American influence) distinguishes most Southern fiddling from any other tradition. This is especially true of Round Peak fiddling. It is vital to master the characteristic rhythms as well as the notes; without that underpinning the tunes just won't sound right. It may seem awkward at first, but as you practice and get a feel for the patterns, the essential flow of the bowing will emerge, and in the long run your fiddling will be more fun and interesting.

It's a matter of style

Keep in mind that the tunes as presented in this book are just examples; there really is no definitive way to play any given tune. What makes a style cohesive—on fiddle, banjo, or anything else—is the way common, familiar elements combine and recombine in ever-shifting but entirely characteristic ways. You need to learn the elements, but you don't always have to put them together the same way. I hope it goes without saying that these examples don't even come close to exhausting the possibilities.

The goal is not just to expand your repertoire, but also to develop a feel for the elements that distinguish traditional fiddling and the ways in which you can creatively combine them. At first you should listen to the accompanying CD and learn the tunes as they're presented here. But gradually you will begin to experiment with different combinations of rhythms and notes, using what you have learned in ways that uniquely suit you. No two people ever sound the same, even if they try; you will inevitably develop an identity as a fiddler as distinct as your own voice or handwriting. Ironically, this is most likely to happen just when you feel you are tapping into something larger than yourself. I've been playing fiddle now for nearly 40 years, and I continue to be amazed by it.

The fiddler's tricks of the trade

"What I tell all these young folks, comes here and wants to learn to play, I tell 'em: That's the hand to watch right there, by gads. Get so you can use that and you'll be all right."
—Tommy Jarrell, commenting on the importance of the bow arm

Bowing

Rhythm is a big part of what makes this music so appealing and fun to play. Bowing is all about rhythm, so mastering it is well worth the effort.

Bow direction is important. Round Peak fiddling is what I call a downbowing style (Tommy called it "pulling your bow"), prevalent throughout the South, in which rhythmic figures and phrases usually begin with a down-bow—although there are plenty of exceptions to this rule of thumb.

Avoid the trap of using a one-rhythm-fits-all approach to bowing. Like other fiddle styles in Southern tradition, Round Peak uses a rich vocabulary of bowing rhythms. The best fiddlers weave them together to create subtleties and textures in a tune. If you pay attention, you'll begin to identify the various rhythms and their permutations as you listen to the tunes. The bowings in this book will give you a stylistically appropriate starting point, but as you become more familiar with the idioms of this particular bowing language, you'll learn to be more flexible and creative in how you employ them.

Alternate tunings

The vast majority of Round Peak fiddle tunes from the turn of the twentieth century are in the keys of A and D, and there are particular tunings for these keys. In addition, there are a number of special tunings that are used more rarely.

The key of A: In A, the fiddle is usually tuned AE'A'E" (the single prime indicates a note in the first octave above middle C, and the double prime indicates a note in the second octave above middle C); in other words, from standard violin tuning you tune both the G and D strings up one whole step.

The key of D: In D, the fiddle is usually tuned AD'A'E"; from standard violin tuning, you tune only the G string up one whole step.

Special tunings: A number of other tunings are used less often: AE'A'C#" for the key of A; DD'A'D" and AD'A'D" for the key of D; GD'A'D" for the key of G; and GD'A'E" for G and other keys. The latter is considered standard by modern fiddlers and violinists, but to Tommy it was unusual and he used it for just a few tunes.

Don't be reluctant to use these alternate tunings. They're essential to getting the right sound. Without the bowed drones and sympathetic ringing of the open strings, you'll lose the flavor that is so crucial to the appeal of this music. You can of course find a way to play the melodies in standard tuning, but the "fiddling" isn't in the melody; it's in the stylistic details, and the use of alternate tunings is part of that package. If your fiddle is healthy, the extra string tension won't hurt it (although it's a good idea to tune your fiddle back to standard pitch when you're through playing), and it doesn't take long to adjust to the new fingerings. The payoff is that you'll get a richer, more traditional sound.

Steel strings

Most traditional Southern fiddlers have used steel strings since they became widely available early in the twentieth century. Modern fiddlers who always play in standard tuning often prefer the warm sound of synthetic strings with a Perlon core. Personally, I like the brightness of steel strings. And when you use the traditional tunings, you'll find steel strings hold their pitch better after retuning, last longer, and are less inclined to break. They're generally less expensive, too.

A flatter bridge

Old-time fiddlers commonly use a flatter arch for the bridge than you'll find on a classical violin. Like much traditional Southern fiddling, Round Peak style involves playing on two or more strings at a time and rocking the bow back and forth to sound the open strings. It's a whole lot easier with a flatter bridge.

Speed

Although I've played the tunes on the accompanying CD more slowly to make them easier to learn, Round Peak dance tunes are typically played quite fast. In the heat of a good music session, Tommy Jarrell often played between 130 and 140 beats per minute. In lower-energy situations, it might be from 120 to 130 bpm. Recordings of Ben Jarrell, his father, are similarly fast. Songs and tunes not used for dancing, such as "Bonaparte's Retreat" and "Sweet Sunny South," would be slower. Practice the tunes slowly at first (with a metronome if necessary) to develop accuracy in technique and timing, and gradually work up to faster speeds. Strong rhythm and good timing are crucial in traditional fiddling, and you should never sacrifice them for speed.

Swing

Most fiddlers play with a slight "swing" which can't really be notated: in a group of four sixteenth notes, the first and third are slightly accented through a combination of greater stress and time value. Fiddlers vary, but normally it's very subtle: equal timing sounds too square, but dotted rhythms are too bouncy. It's somewhere in between. As usual, only your ears can tell you how much is right.

Ornamentation

The old Round Peak style uses many kinds of ornamentation. Special symbols for them are described in the section "Tablature and special symbols."

Grace notes: If you listen to recordings of Tommy carefully, you'll often hear very quick decorative notes played before or between the main notes of a tune. Their timing and emphasis is so subtle and varied that the transcriptions (where they appear in smaller type) give only a crude approximation. Listen to the accompanying CD or to recordings of Tommy to get a sense of how to execute them. They add elegance to the music, but if they give you trouble, you can usually leave them out.

Drone strings: The melody is nearly always accompanied by simultaneously bowing an adjacent open string, like the drone of a bagpipe. In order to avoid cluttering the transcriptions and obscuring the melody line, I usually haven't notated the drones. You have only two choices at most, above or below the melody, so listen to the CD and use your discretion as to what sounds best. Note: There are occasional double stops, where your fingers note two strings simultaneously. These *are* shown in the transcriptions, so just be aware that after a double stop, the open drone string will kick in again even though it isn't shown.

Unisons: These are a kind of drone in which you simultaneously play an open string together with the same note on the string below, for example the open A string and the A note on the D string. You'll use them most often to double the first or last notes of phrases, which often fall on open strings. Unisons are subtle but important, making a rich sound that Tommy described as "the prettiest sound you can get on the fiddle." The transcriptions show where and how to play them.

Slides: Slides are common in Round Peak fiddling. Most often they involve a fairly short, quick slide up to a note from slightly below—a half step or less.

Rocking the bow: Tommy used this term for a technique rarely heard in modern fiddle styles. Other old-timers called it "rolling the bow" or "figure-eight bowing." The bow hand almost never travels in a straight line, but describes circles, eights, and other curlicues in space as it weaves drone strings and double stops together with the melody of the tune. In conjunction with the use of a relatively flat bridge and alternate tunings, bow rocking gets several strings ringing at once, effectively creating a kind of backup to the melody and maximizing resonance and volume. It's a technique that harks back to a time when the fiddle was more of a solo instrument.

The transcriptions can only hint at this rolling motion without becoming cluttered, and in any case it's an imprecise art that can be minimized or exaggerated depending on your mood. Again, let your ears be your guide. Nancy Dols Neithammer made a wonderful video—appropriately called *Bowing Lights*—of Tommy playing in a dark room with a light on his bow hand, and it's the best illustration of the technique I've ever seen. See "Recommended listening, viewing, and reading" in the back of this book for more information.

Catching up the slack: This is Tommy's description of a bow ornament that was widespread among American fiddlers of the 19th century, but which had all but vanished before the middle of the 20th. It sounds almost like a stutter, a quick shuffle at the end of a long downbow. See "Tablature and special symbols" for a more detailed description.

Pulse accents: These are accents that fall midway through a bowstroke, and are executed by bearing down a little harder and faster as the bow keeps moving in the same direction. The bow does not stop and start.

Tune structure and repeats

Fiddlers of Tommy's generation made reference to the high and low parts of a tune, or the fine and coarse parts (referring to the thickness of the strings: the high strings are thin, or "fine," and the low strings are thick, or "coarse"). Tommy liked to describe music as a big wheel, in part because he thought of the structure as being circular. The growing tendency of modern fiddlers to talk about the A and B parts of a tune involves a subtle shift to a linear concept of structure, which implies that one part is the beginning and the other is the end. But traditional fiddlers don't always start or end tunes in the same place, so I find the traditional terminology, which works regardless of where you start, is usually less confusing.

Many old-timers in southwest Virginia and northwest North Carolina had in common with Tommy a relaxed attitude about the structure of tunes. He typically would fiddle the fine part of a tune a set number of times, usually twice, and then stay on the coarse part as long as he felt like it; maybe singing a verse and then playing it a few more times before signaling with a lift of the fiddle that he was going back to the fine part. He also described playing at dances, sitting face-to-face with banjo-picker Charlie Lowe, knees close together. Either could signal the return to the fine part by touching the other's knee with his own.

Variations

Like most traditional old-time fiddling, Round Peak style sticks pretty close to the basic tune. Variations consist mostly of subtle changes in note choice, bowing rhythm, and ornamentation. There's not enough room here to do justice to the range of possibilities, but since tunes are often made of phrases that may differ only slightly, I've tried to show some alternatives in corresponding parts of similar phrases. Swap them around wherever they seem to fit. And again, listen to recordings of fiddlers like Tommy Jarrell to hear how they vary their playing.

Modal tunes

Some of the tunes are what are now commonly called "modal" tunes. This scholarly term wasn't used by any older musicians that I knew. In modern old-time circles, it has come to refer (incorrectly, the scholars will tell you) to tunes based on a scale that's neither major nor minor—for example, one with a flatted seventh scale tone. You don't need to learn about modes unless you're just curious. The key signature will tell you when something odd is going on. Or, just listen and play the tunes the way you hear them. Not all modal tunes are sad or mournful. Many are up-tempo dance tunes, just as high-spirited as anything in a major scale.

Neutral notes

Traditional fiddling uses microtones that fall between the steps of the tempered scale used in most classical and popular music, most often involving a G and/or C that is somewhere between natural and sharp. These aren't mistakes or intonation problems—it's a different aesthetic, and once your ear gets used to the sound, you'll find it adds a special, indispensable flavor to the music. A fretless banjo can get these notes, which is one reason that the fretless was and still is the favored backup instrument in Round Peak music. The tune intros describe which notes to adjust in case you want to try them. Again, use your ears.

Backup chords

When Tommy was learning his music, banjo was the main backup instrument. Round Peak banjo style was not chordal; it was based on melody and drone, just like the fiddle. Guitars and other chording instruments didn't become common in the mountains much before 1920. As you can hear on old recordings, early guitar players mostly stuck with basic I, IV, and V chords and didn't change as often as modern players. The chord structures they superimposed on the often-ambiguous tonality of older fiddle tunes sometimes seem odd to modern sensibilities. You don't have to follow the chords suggested in these transcriptions, but if you want to preserve the traditional character of the music, be sparing with your chord changes and avoid overusing minor chords.

Tablature and special symbols

Tablature ("tab") graphically represents music in terms of what strings to play and where to note them. Tab is intended to supplement your ear, so it'll be more helpful if you first listen to the tune you want to learn on the CD. The music notation in the upper staff can also help clarify elements that are vague in the tab.

The lines and numbers

The four horizontal lines represent the strings, viewed as if the fiddle were on your lap with the lowest string closest to you.

A number on a line shows which finger to use on that string.

In most string instrument tab, the numbers represent frets; but since a fiddle has no frets, it's less confusing to number the fingers. This table shows which finger each number represents, and what the equivalent would be on a fretted instrument (such as a mandolin). Remember: for the tab to work properly, the fiddle must be in the correct tuning.

Fingers 1, 3, and 4 are normally in the same positions in all the tunings. Finger 2 is played either low (close to the second finger), or high (close to the third finger), or occasionally in a neutral position for those "blue" notes or microtones; your can use either your ears or the music notation to determine where it goes.

number in tab	finger to use	equivalent on fretted instrument
0	none	open string
1	index finger	second fret
2	middle finger	third or fourth fret (depending on the key)
3	ring finger	fifth fret
4	pinkie	seventh fret

Bowing

Bowing is indicated with the conventional symbols:

Downbow (bow arm moves away from the fiddle)

Upbow (bow arm moves toward the fiddle)

Note: If you're not used to standard notation, bowing symbols can seem counterintuitive: the upbow symbol looks like it's pointing down, and vice versa, so be careful not to confuse them.

I have not marked every change of bow direction, only enough to keep you on track—usually at the beginnings of phrases. You should change bow direction with each note, except when a note is slurred or tied to the previous note. In that case, continue in the same direction. (See "Slurred notes" and "Ties" below.)

Timing and note duration

Both staffs are divided into measures by vertical bar lines—usually every two taps of your foot (or "beats"), but on rare occasions there will be three or four beats per measure. The duration of notes is shown by conventional symbols in the music notation in the upper staff. If you don't already read music, it's easiest just to listen to the recording to get a sense of the timing, but here's a quick rundown of how the symbols relate to the tapping of your foot:

𝅗𝅥   Hold a half note for two beats.

♩   Hold a quarter note for one beat.

♪   Play two eighth notes per beat. A straight beam replaces the curved flag when they're joined.

♬   Play four sixteenth notes per beat. Two straight beams replace the flags when they're joined.

♩.   A dot next to a note increases its duration by half. This example equals a quarter plus an eighth note.

Grace notes

Grace notes, shown in smaller print than regular notes (see the illustration for "Slurred notes" below for an example), are ornamental notes that are played very quickly. They shouldn't change the timing of the main notes. Listen to the CD to hear what they should sound like. They add elegance to the music, but if they throw you off, you can usually leave them out. It's better to play the basics well than get tripped up in the details.

Slurred notes

A slur is a curved line connecting notes that are played all on one bowstroke. Grace notes that are connected with their own slur to the beginning or end of a group of slurred notes should be played on the same bowstroke with the others.

    A dashed line means the slur is optional: you can play the notes all together, or on separate bow-strokes.

Ties

A tie is a curved line, like a slur, but it connects two notes of the same pitch. Play just one note and hold it for the combined time of the two notes. This happens most often when a note is held across a bar line.

    I also use a tie when there's a pulse accent on the second note (see "Pulse accents" below).

Repeats

A symbol that look like a colon (:) marks both the beginning and end of a part to be repeated.

Slides

A slanted line (/) in front of a note means you slide into it. $\overline{\underline{\diagup 2}}$

    There's no significance to the length or angle of the line. Most slides are upwards and begin less than a half step below the ending note. There are specific instructions in the transcriptions for anything different.

"Catching up the slack"

I use *"cs"* to mark an optional bow ornament used by many older fiddlers, including Tommy Jarrell (who called it "catching up the slack"). You can either play it as written:

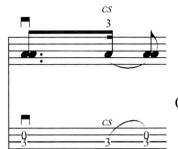

Or, with the ornament, it would sound like this:

Examples on the CD will give you a better sense of what they should sound like.

Pulse accents

Pulse accents usually occur on an upbow, and are marked with a symbol that looks like a "greater than" sign (>); it resembles an upbow symbol on its side, so be careful not to confuse the two. I show pulse accents as two notes tied together, with the accent on the second note. Keep the bow moving in the same direction, and push a little faster and bear down a little harder for the second note. The bow shouldn't stop and start.

Plucking the strings

This is what violinists call "left-hand pizzicato." It's marked with a symbol that looks like a plus sign (+). Pluck the open string with a finger of your noting hand (not your bowing hand). I like to use my ring finger, but use whichever works best for you.

Brad Leftwich

Tommy Jarrell's birthplace in Round Peak; Fisher's Peak rises in the background

AE'A'E" tuning (key of A)

1. Baby-o 💿

Tommy learned this tune from his father and uncle, Ben and Charlie Jarrell. About the words to the song, Tommy remarked, "I reckon he must have been a mean baby."

The baby this and the baby that
The baby killed my old tomcat

Chorus:
What're you gonna do with the baby?
What're you gonna do with the baby-o?

Wrap him up in the table cloth
We'll put him up in the stable loft

Wrap him up in calico
We'll smack his bottom and let him go

The baby laughed, the baby cried
I stuck my finger in the baby's eye

2. Big-Eyed Rabbit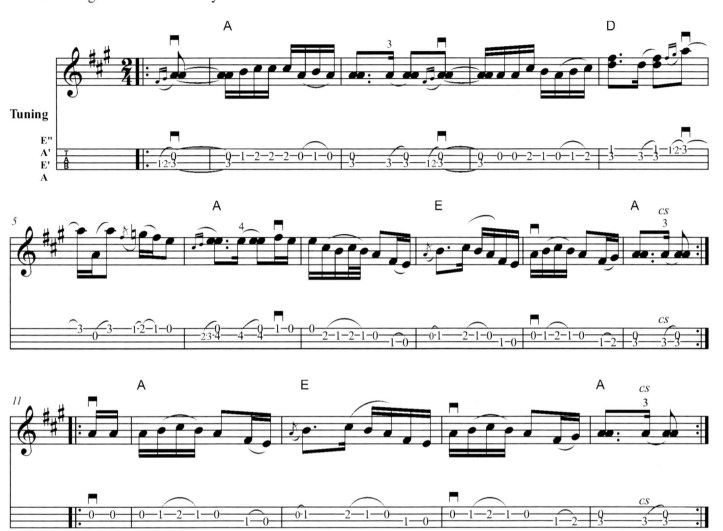

Versions of this old tune, which Tommy learned from his father, are fairly common in the area. Some are nearly indistinguishable from the bluegrass standard "Pig in a Pen." The evocative image of "rocking in a weary land" turns up occasionally in other songs and tunes, and probably comes indirectly from Isaiah 32:2: "And a man shall be as an hiding place from the wind, and a covert from the tempest; as rivers of water in a dry place, as the shadow of a great rock in a weary land."

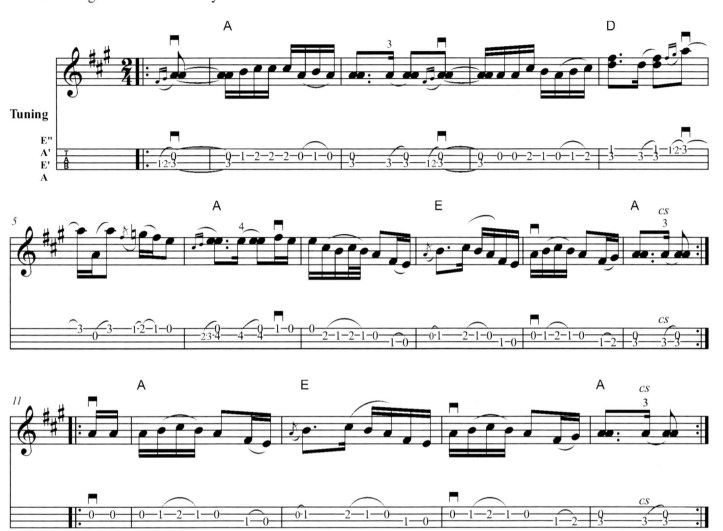

Yonder comes a rabbit
Skipping through the sand
Shoot that rabbit, he don't mind
Fry him in my pan, Lord
I'll fry him in my pan

Chorus 1:
Big-eyed rabbit's gone, gone
The big-eyed rabbit's gone

Yonder comes a rabbit
Just hard as he can run
It's yonder comes another one
Gonna shoot 'em with a double-barrel gun, gun
Shoot 'em with a double-barrel gun

Yonder comes my darling
It's how do you know?
I know her by her pretty blue eyes
Shining bright like gold
Shining bright like gold

Chorus 2:
I'm rocking in a weary land
I'm rocking in a weary land

19

3. The Blackest Crow (My Dearest Sweetheart)

Tommy told me, "I learned that tune from a fellow by the name of Jake Norman, first man ever I heard pick it on the banjo. He wasn't much of a banjo picker, but he could play that tune. And then I heard my mother sing it. It's an old ballad, you know, it's, I forget, 200 years old, probably more than that."

The time draws near, my dearest dear, when you and I must part
But little do you know of the grief and woe of my poor aching heart
It's what I suffer for your sake, you're the one I love so dear
I wish that I was going with you, or you were staying here

I wish my breast was made of glass, wherein you might behold
For there your name lies wrote, my dear, in letters made of gold
For there your name lies wrote my dear, believe me what I say
You are the one I love the best until my dying day

The crow that is so black, my love, will surely turn to white
If ever I prove false to you, bright day may turn to night
Bright day may turn to night, my love, the elements may mourn
If ever I prove false to you, the sea may rage and burn

I wish that you and me, my love, were on yonder shady rock
And we had neither wealth nor care, and riches was forgot
I'd wish for every day a week, and every week a year
How happy, happy would I be in the presence of you, dear

Jake Norman (1874-*c*1934)

Jake, the man from whom Tommy learned "The Blackest Crow," lived on Round Peak Church Road along with his father, Calvin, and his brothers, Dixie and Alex. All four were banjo pickers. In contrast to what Tommy said about Jake's music, it's worth noting that Dick Freeman, another Round Peak banjo player and Tommy's contemporary, described Jake as a "*good* banjo picker!" In addition to his skills on the banjo, Jake was described as a great flatfoot dancer. His brother Dixie, who also played "The Blackest Crow," is remembered as one of the best dance callers in the area.

4. Breaking up Christmas

This much-played tune refers to a mountain holiday tradition in which dances were held in different homes in the community over a period of two weeks, beginning the day after Christmas. They would begin in the afternoon, break for supper, and often continue late into the night. Paul Sutphin said that Pet McKinney was the main source for this tune in the Round Peak area. It was played across the mountain in Virginia, as well.

Variation on the low part:

Tommy sang these three verses, and claimed authorship of the last two:

Hooray Jake, hooray John
Breaking up Christmas all night long

Way back yonder, a long time ago
The old folks danced the do-si-do

Santa Claus come, done and gone
Breaking up Christmas right along

5. Chilly Winds

Banjo picker Carlie Holder (1896–1971) showed Tommy this tune during a break at a dance they were playing around 1916. Tommy advised me, "Don't never put your first finger down, or you'll make a mess of it."
The C and G notes should be neutral: sharp of natural, but not actual sharps. They give the melody a hair-raising, lonesome edge that is lost when you use a conventionally tuned A minor scale. Area guitar players would use A and E major chords to back it up, further enhancing the tension between major and minor.

6. Cluck Old Hen

Ben Jarrell played this tune, but it was neighbor Tony Lowe who inspired Tommy to learn it: "At a school breaking, Tony did the first trick fiddling ever I seen. He swung his fiddle out and plucked those strings playing 'Cluck Old Hen,' keeping perfect time all the while." (For more on school breakings, see "Peek-a-boo," p. 88.) Note the key signature: the Round Peak setting for this tune is the key of A with a lowered seventh scale tone, hence two sharps. Actually, Tommy played a neutral G, slightly sharp of natural, giving the tune a bluesy feel.

My old hen's a good old hen
She lays eggs for the railroad men
Sometimes one, sometimes two
Sometimes enough for the whole dang crew

Cluck old hen, cluck I said
Cluck old hen, your widdies* all dead

I had an old hen, she had a wooden leg
The best dang hen that ever laid an egg

She laid more eggs than the hens around the barn
Another little drink wouldn't do me no harm

Cluck old hen, cluck for your corn
Cluck old hen, your widdies all gone

Cluck old hen, cluck in the lot
Next time you cluck, you'll cluck in the pot

* "Widdies" are baby chicks.

24

Tommy Jarrell's fiddle

How Tommy got his fiddle

Tommy told Nancy Dols Neithammer: "There come an epidemic of that typhoid fever up there in our country [in 1911]. I had a little touch of it, and there was several folks died with it, and Tony [Lowe] was one of them that died. And him and Daddy fiddled a lot together, you know. We lived in one holler and they lived just over in the other. And after a while, after Tony died, his widow come over there and says, 'Ben, I know Tony'd rather you'd have his fiddle than anybody. I need a little money, and I want to sell it to you.' Daddy said, 'Mae, what do you want for the fiddle?' She says, 'I want five dollars.' Well, Daddy bought the fiddle.

"I'd just started learning on it, you know, and Houston Moore, my mother's first cousin, come up there one time, him and his wife, stayed all night with us, and he brought this [other] fiddle, you know. Well, Daddy had the Tony Lowe fiddle, and he'd play first one fiddle and then he'd play the other one, and they sounded so much alike, you know. I couldn't tell the difference in the sound of them.

"Well, [the Tony Lowe fiddle] come unglued back there at the neck, and Daddy sent it down here to Mount Airy to have it repaired, never did see the fiddle no more. I was beginning to learn a little on it, you know, and so I wanted that Houston Moore fiddle, 'cause it sounded so much like the one I'd learned on. So I went and borrowed ten dollars from Ed Ward, went down and I found out what Houston wanted for the fiddle, and I went down there and bought it, give him ten dollars for it. That's how come me with the fiddle. I bought it when I was fourteen years old, 1915. And I've had it ever since.

"I like to never got that fiddle paid for, I'd pay but a dollar or two at a time. Finally my daddy asked me one time, he said, 'How much you still owe on your fiddle, Tommy?' I said, 'Oh, two dollars and a half.' And he just run his hand in his pocket and handed me two dollars and a half, said, 'Go pay it off.' But you know, money was hard to get ahold of, by gosh, when I was fourteen years old."

7. Cotton-Eyed Joe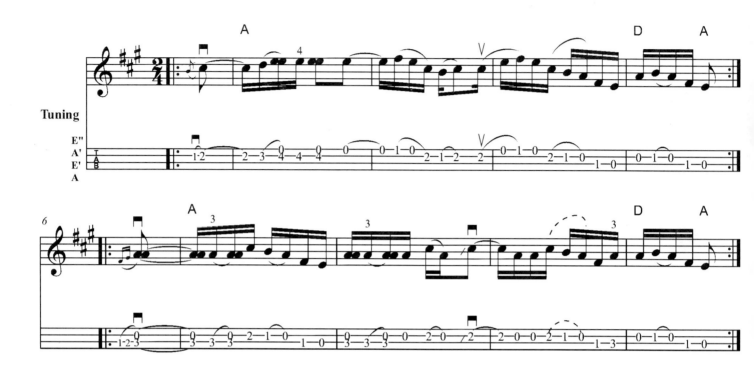

Tommy said there was an old-time version of this tune, but I don't know that he ever played it. He learned this one from Charlie Lowe, who heard it on a radio broadcast sometime after 1925.

Courtesy Reavis Lyons

Charlie Lowe (on right) with Tommy Jarrell

Eighteen, nineteen, twenty years ago
Daddy had a man called Cotton-Eyed Joe

Chorus:
Where'd you come from, where'd you go?
Where'd you come from, Cotton-Eyed Joe?

He made him a fiddle and he made him a bow
And he made a little tune called Cotton-Eyed Joe

Cornstalk fiddle and a shoestring bow
And he played that tune called Cotton-Eyed Joe

You can hang up your fiddle and hang up your bow
Old Joe's gone where the good folks go

Charlie Lowe (1878–1964)

The most respected banjo player of Round Peak, Charlie was Tommy's playing partner for nearly 50 years and had an enormous influence on musicians in the area. Charlie cultivated the local music scene, encouraging young people who wanted to play music, arranging for them to get instruments, and giving them opportunities to play at dances and other social events. He played for countless dances, but he wouldn't put up with disturbances caused by drinking and fighting. If trouble started he'd pack up his instruments and leave. His daughter Mary Jane Faulkner recalls that there was music in the house constantly: "He'd start playing every night after supper until bedtime, then he'd wake us up playing the banjo in the morning." His generosity was legendary. Tommy said, "You go to Charlie Lowe's house when it come eating time and you had to eat… He was willing to divide whatever he had with anybody. Wasn't no better feller than Charlie Lowe."

26

8. Cripple Creek

Tommy noted with disapproval that "most people put a little 'Greasy String' in there," referring to the end of the first phrase in the low part (measure 12). Here's what he thought was the correct way to play "Cripple Creek." (Have a look at "Greasy String," p. 32, for comparison.)

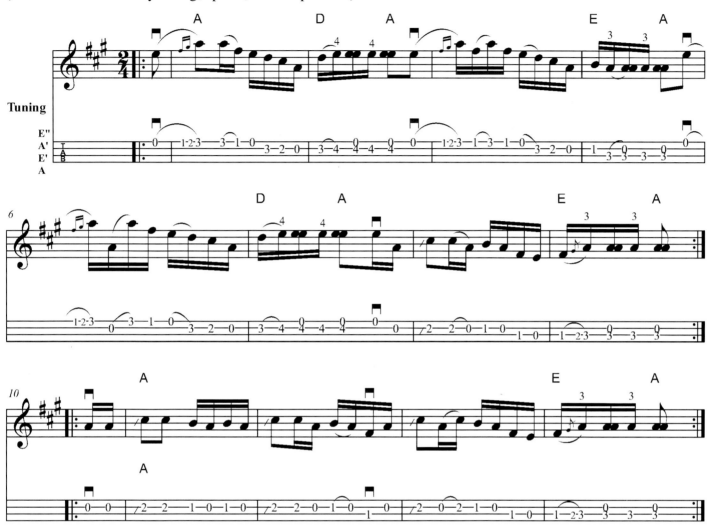

Roll my britches up to my knees
Wade old Cripple Creek where I please

Oh me, oh my
Gonna wade old Cripple Creek till I die

Going up Cripple Creek, going in a run
Going up Cripple Creek to have a little fun

Going up Cripple Creek, going all right
Going up Cripple Creek Saturday night

Going up Cripple Creek, going in a whirl
Going up Cripple Creek to see my girl

Gals up Cripple Creek a-laying in the shade
Getting all the money that a poor boy's made

Gals up Cripple Creek about half grown
They jump on the boys like a dog on a bone

9. Darling Nellie Grey

Written by Benjamin Hanby in 1856, this song entered oral tradition and was widely played and sung in the mountains. In the Round Peak community, Boggie Cockerham (see p. 55) was known for playing the tune. Kyle Creed learned it from him, and it became one of Kyle's signature pieces on banjo.

28

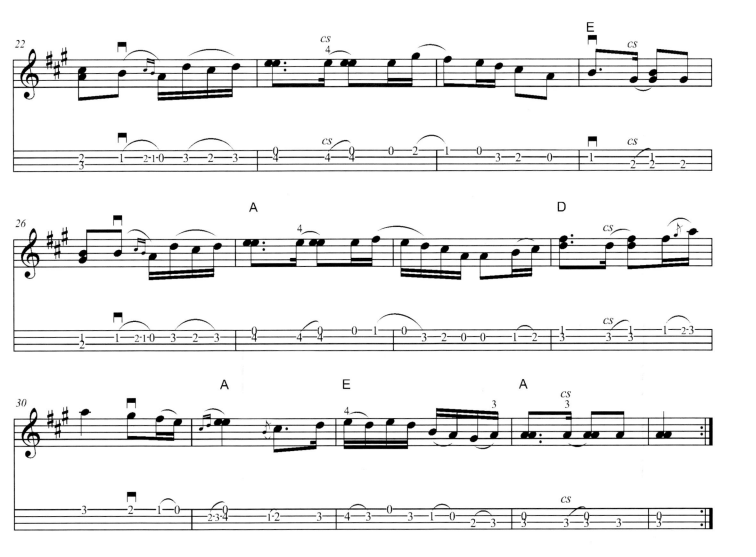

There's a low green valley on the old Kentucky shore
Where I've whiled many happy hours away
A-sitting and a-singing by the little cabin door
Where lived my darling Nellie Grey

Chorus:
Oh my darling Nellie Grey, they have taken you away
And I'll never get to see you anymore
I'm sitting by the river and so lonely all the day
For you've gone from the old Kentucky shore

When the moon had climbed the mountain
    and the stars were shining too
Then I'd take my darling Nellie Grey
And we'd float down the river in my little red canoe
And my banjo sweetly I would play

One night I went to see her,
    but she's gone the neighbors say
The white man bound her with his chain
They have taken her to Georgia to wear her life away
As she toils in the cotton and the cane

My canoe is under water and my banjo is unstrung
And I'm tired of living anymore
My eyes shall look downward and my song shall be
    unsung
While I stay on the old Kentucky shore

My eyes are getting blinded and I cannot see my way
Hark! There's somebody knocking at the door
I hear the angels calling and I see my Nellie Grey
Farewell to the old Kentucky shore

Last chorus:
Oh my darling nellie Grey, up in heaven there they say
That they'll never take you from me anymore
I am coming, I am coming as the angels clear the way
Farewell to the old Kentucky shore

29

10. Fire on the Mountain

This probably came to Tommy from his uncle Charlie Jarrell, who, according to Paul Sutphin, played the tune and taught it to Kyle Creed as well.

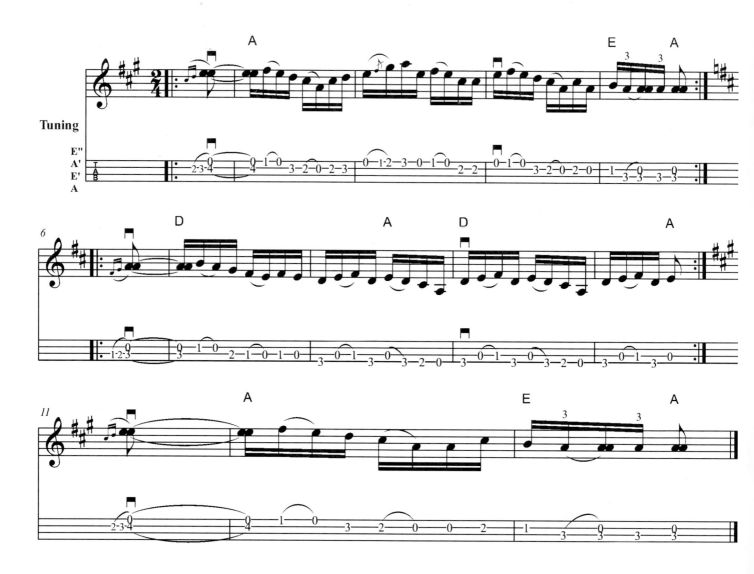

11. Granny, Will Your Dog Bite?

Although he would play this on request, Tommy wasn't really comfortable with it. He protested, "I've heard that tune years ago, but I never did play it. Charlie Lowe used to all the time get me to try to play it." Tommy's intonation tended to be a little sharp of G natural in the high part.

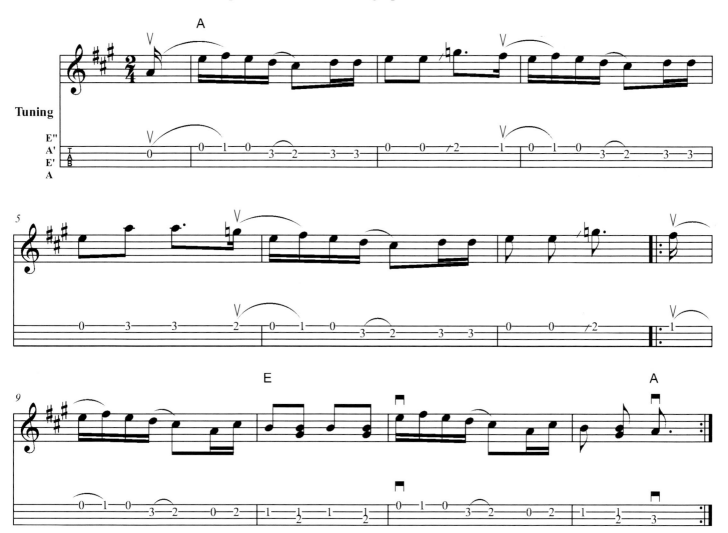

Granny, will your dog bite, dog bite, dog bite?
Granny, will your dog bite? No, child, no.

31

12. Greasy String

Tommy's uncle Charlie Jarrell was the only fiddler he ever heard play this one, but there are recordings of Norman Edmonds of Carroll County, Va., playing it, and doubtless other fiddlers in the area did as well. Tunes named "Greasy String" are played at least as far away as West Virginia and can be quite different from one another. A greasy fiddle string will whistle and squawk, like a jay or catbird; even so, the words to this tune are enigmatic to say the least. Tommy noted that this is one of just a few tunes where he would start phrases on an upbow. But there's a lot more going on than just that. The bowing is a masterpiece of rhythmic complexity.

Run little feet, stop and sing
Mash down harder on the greasy string

Jaybird whistle and the catbird sing
Mash down harder on the greasy string

My old lady, she's mad at me
Because I won't drink ginger tea
She is good, and she is bad
She gives me the devil when she gets mad

32

Charlie Jarrell

Making beautiful music together

Charlie Jarrell (see profile on p. 8) fiddled regularly with banjo player Cyrus Lawson at dances, but making good music together didn't mean they always got along. Cyrus told Kevin Donleavy, "Charlie could play a fiddle pretty well. But if you didn't have your banjo tuned just the way he wanted it, he'd try to take your banjo away from you and tune it. He got hold of it one time, and I said, 'I'm going to punch you in the damn nose!' And I'd have done it, too. He was an old slim fellah. He commenced for to grab it out of my hand. I said, 'Listen here! Damned if I won't hit you in the head with it!' He could be as mean as a striped snake."

Dick Freeman commented on that rocky musical relationship: "Those old fiddlers—you didn't get in front of them! You stayed behind them. Charlie Jarrell used to hit Cyrus Lawson with his fiddle bow, saying, 'Get back there, boy!'"

13. Groundhog

Tommy's rhythmic refrain of nonsense syllables is a little unusual and a lot of fun to sing. He objected to what he called the Nashville way of singing a drawn-out "ground-hog" for the refrain: "That don't finish it up like it ought to be," he'd say. "'Yank-a-tum-a-yank-a-tum-a-yay,' now that finishes it up."

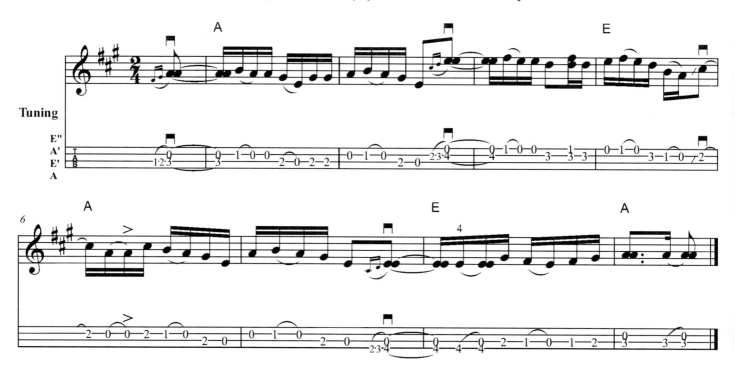

Shoulder up my gun, whistle up my dog [2 times]
Going in the mountains, gonna catch a groundhog

Refrain:
Yank-a-tum-a-yank-a-tum-a-yay
[or sometimes: Yim-a-tum-a-yank-a-tum-a-yay]

Whistle up my dog, shoulder up my gun
Going in the mountains, gonna have a little fun

I run him in the rock, I run him in the cleft
Great big groundhog, bigger'n I can lift

I run him in the rock, I run him in the log
Good God a-mighty, what a big groundhog

I pulled out my knife and skinned one side
Good God a-mighty, what a groundhog hide

Yonder comes grandad popping his cane
Swearing he'll eat that groundhog brain

Yonder come Sal with a snicker and a grin
Goundhog gravy all over her chin

The young'uns all kicked, they squealed and cried
They do love goundhog stewed and fried

Two little pigs and one old sow
Who are happier than we are now

14. Ida Red

Also known as "Down the Road," this tune is played widely throughout the South, at least as far west as Texas. Some Galax-area musicians played it in the key of D, but Tommy preferred it in A. "I put that to it, about Santa Claus washing his feet," he claimed.

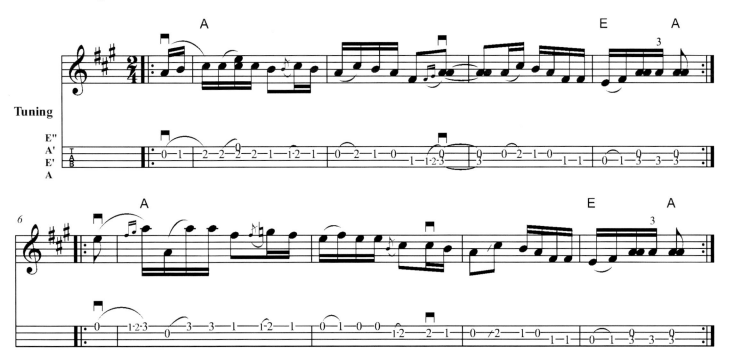

Up the road and down the road
All my people live down the road

Ida Red, she ain't no fool
She can ride astraddle of a humpback mule

Ida Red, she comes to town
Riding a billygoat and leading a hound

Down the road and across the creek
See old Santa Claus a-washing his feet

Ida Red, Ida Green
Prettiest little gal I've ever seen

Ida Red, Ida blue
I got stuck on Ida, too

15. John Brown's Dream

Charlie Lowe and Ben Jarrell made this tune by revamping an older tune, "Pretty Little Girl." You can hear Ben play it with DaCosta Woltz's Southern Broadcasters, who recorded for Gennett in 1927. Tommy loved to play it and would spin off seemingly endless rhythmic variations down on the low strings.

36

Tommy usually played a number of low variations on the third part before starting over. Here's three:

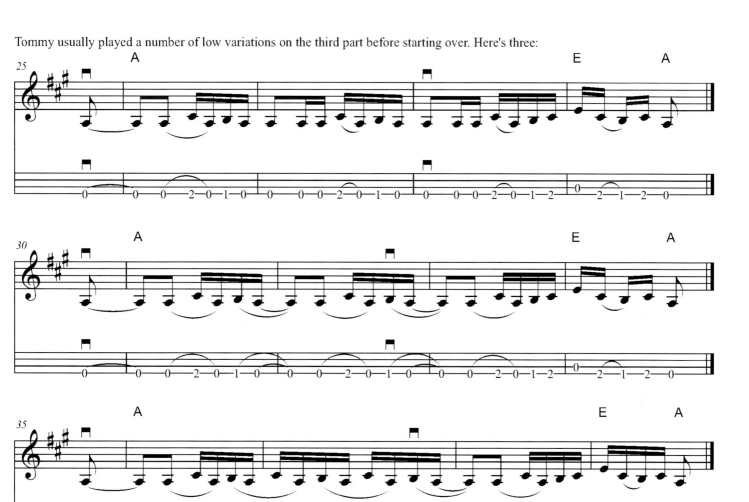

Sung on the second part:
John Brown dreamed,
John Brown dreamed, the devil was dead

Sung on the third part:
Come on Lula, come on Lula
Come on Lula, with your hog and your bread

Sung on the second part:
Soon be time,
Soon be time to cook and eat again

Sung on the third part:
Boating up Cindy, Cindy, Cindy
Boating up Cindy, how do you do?

Sung on the third part:
I'm gonna marry, I'm gonna marry
I'm gonna marry that pretty little girl

16. John Hardy

John Hardy was hanged for murder in McDowell County, West Virginia, on January 19, 1894. He supposedly made the song himself and sang it on the scaffold before his execution. Tommy actually used a neutral G note in the low part rather than a G-natural which, along with the slide to the C-sharp, gives it a bluesy character that distinguishes it from modern bluegrass versions.

Tommy's first verse to "John Hardy" combines parts of verses that are distinct in most versions, and in doing so omits the detail that Hardy killed a man in a crap game at Shawnee Camp (locale of the Shawnee Coal Company). Tommy was unaware the song was based on actual events. "It's just an old song," he said.

John Hardy, he was a wild, cruel man
He carried two guns every day
He shot the conductor on the northbound train
And they put John Hardy back in jail, poor boy
Put John Hardy back in jail

John Hardy, he went to the old barroom
And he got so drunk he could not see
Along come the sheriff and grabs him by the arm
John Hardy come and go along with me, poor boy
John Hardy come and go along with me

He's been to the East and he's been to the West
He's been this whole world all around
He's been to the river and he's been baptized
But now he's on his burying ground, poor boy
Now he's on his burying ground

John Hardy had a wife and she lived in the West
She was always dressed in blue
And when she heard John Hardy was dead
John Hardy, I've been true to you, poor boy
John Hardy, I've been true to you

Oh, they dug his grave with a silver spade
A gold chain to let him down
His friends and relatives all standing around
When they laid him in the cold, damp ground, poor boy
When they laid him in the cold, damp ground

17. John Henry

Tommy said, "That come from Allegheny County, over the mountain. Uncle Charlie Jarrell, he was a moonshiner. He was over there making whiskey when I was about 15 years old. He come back home, and 'By God, Tommy' he said, 'I've learned a new tune… It's old "John Henry."' And he had me to get the banjer, and that's the way he played it." Charlie's version with its distinctive high part became the Round Peak standard.

18. June Apple

Tommy first learned "June Apple" on banjo, backing up his father's fiddling. As in "Cluck Old Hen," Tommy actually played a neutral G note throughout, between natural and sharp, and a bluesy slide up to it in the high part. Most area guitar players play A, D, and E major chords behind the tune.

I wish I was a June apple, hanging on a tree
Every time my true love passed, she'd take a little bite of me

I'm going across the mountain, I'm going in the spring
When I get on the other side, I'm gonna hear my woman sing

Don't you hear the banjo sing, I wish that gal was mine?
Can't you hear the banjo sing, I wish that gal was mine?

Charlie he's a nice young man, Charlie he's a dandy
Charlie he's a nice young man, he feeds the gals on candy

Over the river to feed my sheep, over the river Charlie
Over the river to feed my sheep, to feed them on barley

I wish I had some sticks and poles to build my chimley [chimney] higher
Every time it rains or snows, it puts out all my fire

41

19. Kitty Clyde (Katy Cline)

Another tune that Tommy learned from his father, this is a local version of the mountain love song "I'm as Free a Little Bird as I Can Be."

Oh, I wish I was a little bee, a honeybee
I'd never gather honey from the flower
I would steal just one kiss from my sweet Kitty's lips
And I'd build my hive on her brow

Chorus:
Oh say, do you love me Kitty Clyde, Kitty Clyde
Oh say, do you love me Kitty Clyde?
Say, do you love me, my sweet little girl
Oh say, do you love me Kitty Clyde?

Oh, I wish I was a little fish, a little fish
I'd never bite the hook nor the line
I would swim, I would swim to the middle of the sea
And I'd leave all them big fish behind

Oh, I wish I was a little dove, a turtledove
I would fly far over the sea
I would fly, I would fly, but I never would return
Till my sweetheart sent for me

42

20. Let Me Fall (Old Hard Road) 🎧

Charlie Barnett Lowe (see p. 103) lived beyond Toenail Gap in Carroll County, Va. His daughter Sel reminisced, "In the wintertime he would get up before daylight. After breakfast, he'd sit and pick the banjo. Then he would go to the barn to feed the teams, going off singing 'Let Me Fall.' I can just hear him. He never did sing much with the banjo but he would go down the path to the barn singing that one." Ben Jarrell (who called it "Old Hard Road") and Charlie played the tune at a dance at a corn shucking, where Tommy, about 21 or 22 at the time, learned it.

If I get drunk, if I get drunk
Just let me fall, little darling, on the ground

On the ground, on the ground
Just let me fall, little darling, on the ground

Oh me, oh my
Let me fall, let me fall, let me fall

Lay me down, lay me down
Lay me down, little darling, on the ground

Weep and moan, weep and moan
Carry me home, little darling, carry me home

Old hard road, old hard road
Kill me dead, kill me dead, kill me dead

Tie my shoes, tie my shoes
If I get drunk, little girl, tie my shoes

43

21. Little Maggie

Tommy had just learned this tune about 1916 when his cousin Julie was fatally burned trying to revive the fire in a wood cook stove by pouring kerosene onto it. He told Ray Alden, "When I reached the door I saw Aunt Susan kneeling above Julie, weeping, her hands all blistered from beating out the fire on her with a quilt. They put Julie to bed right away. Her whole body was burned up to her chin, and at first she cried in pain, but after a while she didn't feel anything at all. As she was a-laying there she asked me to get my banjo and sing 'Little Maggie' for her… It seemed to comfort her and pick up her spirits a little, but by the following morning she was dead." Author Charles Frazier adapted Tommy's account of the event and used it in his novel *Cold Mountain*.

Although the key signature shows two sharps, Tommy actually played a neutral G rather than a G natural.

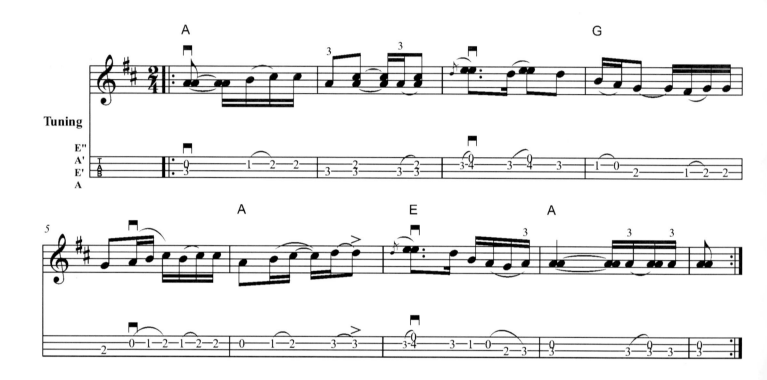

Oh, it's yonder stands little Maggie, got a dram glass in her hand
She's a-drinking to drown her troubles, and courting another man

Oh, it's how can I ever stand it, to see them two blue eyes
Shining like some diamonds, pretty diamonds in the sky

Come and go with me to the depot, got a suitcase in my hand
Lord, I'm going away and leave you, you can hunt you another man*

Oh, the last time I saw little Maggie, she was sitting on the banks of the sea
Had the whiskey bottles all stacked all around her, and a banjo upon her knee

Pretty flowers they're made for blooming, pretty stars they're made to shine
Pretty girls they're made for loving, and little Maggie was made for mine

Oh, I'd rather be off in some dark hollow, where the sun don't never shine
Than to think that you love some other, won't be no little darling of mine

Go away, go away, little Maggie, go and leave just as fast as you can
Gonna hunt me another woman, like you got you another man

* Sometimes Tommy sang: "…I'm going to some far distant land"

44

22. Lonesome Road Blues 💿

This song became popular in the area when Tommy was young. Another song in the local repertoire often called "Lonesome Road" became "Fall on My Knees"(p. 76) to accommodate it.

Tuning

2nd finger slide
from B to C#

As a variation, this phrase can
be played an octave lower

I'm going down this long, lonesome road
Yes, I'm going down this long, lonesome road
Going down this long, lonesome road
Lord, I ain't gonna be treated this-a-way

Oh, I'm way down in jail on my knees
Lord, I'm way down in jail on my knees
Oh, I'm way down in jail on my knees
Lord, they feed me on cornbread and peas

Oh, it's Mama won't buy me no shoes
No, Mama won't buy me no shoes

No, Mama won't buy me no shoes
Lord, I ain't gonna be treated this-a-way

Oh, that sweet-talking don't do my baby no good
No, sweet-talking don't do my baby no good
Oh, sweet-talking don't do my baby no good
I'd go back and see her if I could

Oh, I'm going where the chilly winds don't blow
Oh, I'm going where the climate suits my clothes
I'm going where the chilly winds don't blow
And I ain't gonna be treated this-a-way

45

23. Old Bunch of Keys

"That's about the best tune to dance them old-timey reels to, like the Half Moon," Tommy said. "That came from across the mountain, near Fancy Gap." Tommy learned the tune in the early 1920s when he went with Charlie Barnett Lowe to visit two fiddlers from that area Charlie often played music with, Fred Hawks and John Rector. John himself had learned the tune from "old man Marcus Hanks" (1857-1936), who neighbors remembered as much for his explosive temper as his fiddling.

Tommy consistently used a neutral G in this tune, slightly sharp of natural.

24. Old Joe Clark

Tommy learned this tune from his father, who recorded it with the Southern Broadcasters in 1927. As with other A tunes I've transcribed with two sharps, Tommy actually used a scale with a neutral G.

I don't like old Joe Clark, I'll tell you the reason why
He run through my field the other day and he tore down all my rye

Old Joe Clark's a fine old man, a-courting Betty Brown
Old Joe Clark's a fine old man, from the top of the house on down

Don't never marry an old maid, boys, I'll tell you the reason why
Her legs so long and stringy, I'm afraid she'll never die

I went over to old Joe's house, he's standing in the door
His shoes and stockings in his hand, his feet all over the floor

I used to live on the mountainside, but now I live in town
A-boarding at a big hotel and courting Betty Brown

25. Police

Charlie Jarrell learned this tune in his travels across the mountain and brought it to Round Peak. The words fit the tune much better if you follow local usage and pronounce it "PO-lice." I've changed some offensive words.

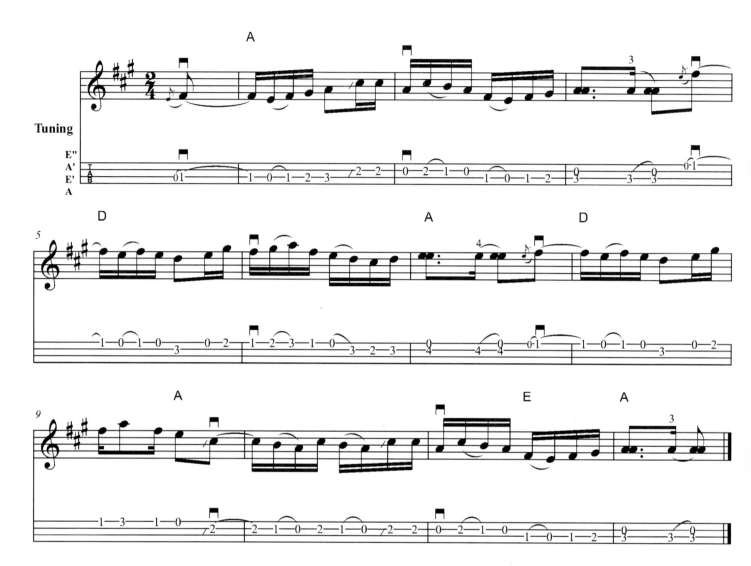

Police come, I didn't want to go this morning
Police come, I didn't want to go this morning
Police come, I didn't want to go
Shot him in the head with my 44 this morning

Bullfrog jumped from bank to bank this morning
Bullfrog jumped from bank to bank this morning
Bullfrog jumped from bank to bank
Skinned his whole back from shank to shank
  this morning

Two little children laying in the bed this morning
Two little children laying in the bed this morning
Two little children laying in the bed
One rolled over to the other and said it's morning

I know something I ain't gonna tell this morning
I know something I ain't gonna tell this morning
I know something I ain't gonna tell
I want to go to heaven in a coconut shell this morning

Great big fellow laying on a log this morning
Great big fellow laying on a log this morning
Great big fellow laying on a log
Finger on the trigger and his eye on the hog
  this morning

Down went the trigger and bang went the gun
  this morning
Down went the trigger and bang went the gun
  this morning
Down went the trigger and bang went the gun
Wish I had a wagon to haul him home this morning

48

26. Poor Ellen Smith

Peter DeGraff murdered Ellen Smith in nearby Forsyth County on July 20, 1892, and was tried and hanged in Winston (now Winston-Salem) on February 8, 1894. DeGraff supposedly wrote the song himself and set it to the hymn tune "How Firm a Foundation." Tommy said his father, who would have been about 14 at the time, went to Winston during the trial and returned with the song.

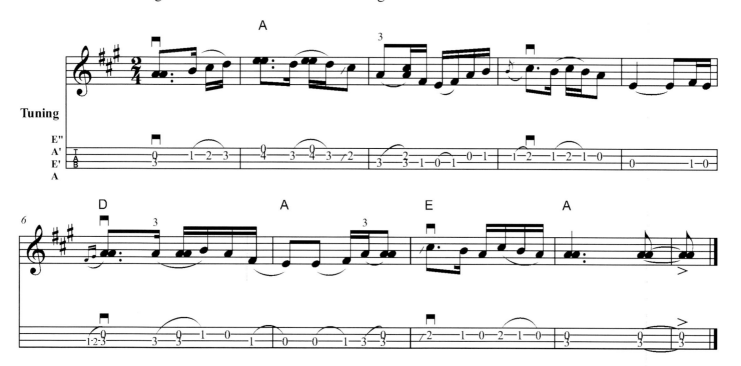

Poor Ellen Smith, and it's how she was found
She was shot through the heart, lying cold on the ground

Oh, I hushed back my tears when the people all said
That Peter DeGraff had shot Ellen Smith dead

While I would have never made her my wife
Lord, I loved her too dearly to take her sweet life

They grabbed their Winchesters, they hunted me down
While I was away in old Mount Airy town

They carried me to Winston, my trial to stand
To live or to die as the law makes a man [may command]

McArthur will hang me, he will if he can
God knows if they hang me, I'll die an innocent man

27. Pretty Little Girl 🔆

Ben Jarrell and Charlie Lowe overhauled this old tune to create a new one they called "John Brown's Dream," although that is also a common alternate name for "Pretty Little Girl." Fred Cockerham always maintained the two tunes were the same, but the souped-up Jarrell-Lowe version of "John Brown's Dream" is substantially different from "Pretty Little Girl."

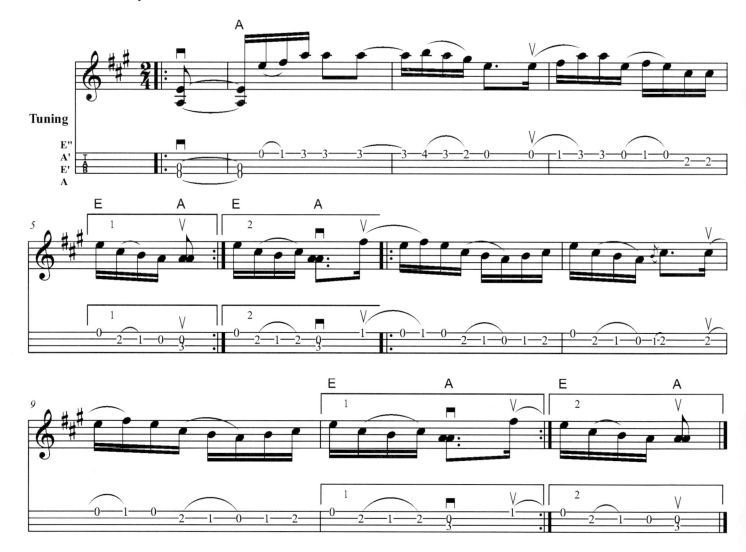

Who's been here since I've been gone?
A pretty little girl with a red dress on

I'm gonna marry that pretty little girl
I'm gonna marry that pretty little girl

I'm gonna get that pretty little girl
I'm gonna get that pretty little girl

28. Pretty Polly

Tommy's bowing on this classic mountain murder ballad was not at all like his dance tunes or even most of his songs. Like "When Sorrows Encompass Me Round" and "Chilly Winds," this is not a true A minor scale; Tommy played both C and G as neutral tones, halfway between natural and sharp, giving the tune an edge that a minor scale can't duplicate.

Pretty Polly, pretty Polly, come go along with me [2 times]
Before we get married, some pleasure we'll see

She climbed up behind him and away they did go
Over the hills and the valley so low

Oh, they went up a little farther and what did they spy
A new-dug grave and a spade lying by

Oh Willie, oh Willie, I'm afraid of your way
I'm afraid that you'll lead my poor body astray

Oh Polly, oh Polly, your guess is about right
I dug on your grave the biggest part of last night

He stabbed her to the heart and her life blood did flow
And into the grave pretty Polly did go

He threw some dirt over her and turned to go home
While the wild birds and the turtledoves were left to mourn

29. Rainbow Sign 💿

The Carter Family popularized this song in the late 1920s. Tommy, a former moonshiner, sang with particular gusto the verses about Noah and his wine. "You can look in the Bible," he said, "it's right there in Genesis."

God gave Noah the rainbow sign, don't you see? [2 times]
God gave Noah the rainbow sign
No more water but the fire next time
Hide me, oh rock of ages, cleft for me

Poor old Lazarus, poor as I, don't you see?
Poor old Lazarus, poor as I
When he died he had a home on high
Hide me, oh rock of ages, cleft for me

From east to west the fire might roll, hide thou me
East to west the fire might roll
Lord have mercy on my poor soul
Hide me, oh rock of ages, cleft for me

Old Noah planted him a vinyard, don't you see?
Old Noah planted him a vine
And commenced to make a little wine
Hide me, oh rock of ages, cleft for me

Poor old Noah drank a little wine, don't you see?	Oh, there's honey in that rock, don't you see?
Poor old Noah drank a little wine	Oh, there's honey in that rock
He got high as a Georgia pine	Way up on the mountaintop
Hide me, oh rock of ages, cleft for me	Hide me, oh rock of ages, cleft for me

30. Round Town Gals (Buffalo Gals)

This is the Round Peak version of the old minstrel tune "Buffalo Gals."

Round town gals, won't you come out tonight
Come out tonight, come out tonight?
Round town gals, won't you come out tonight
And dance by the light of the moon?

31. Ruben

This was Tommy's first tune, learned on banjo at age seven or eight from Boggie Cockerham, who was helping the Jarrells with their farmwork. He told Nancy Dols Neithammer, "[Boggie] was paid by the month, hired for a year to make a crop. And we was a-minding the old steers, out of the corn down in the meadow there, letting them graze. Boggie plowed, worked them, you know—had to let them eat some, 12 o'clock. And he tuned the banjo down for old 'Ruben.' He handed it over to me, said, 'Here, Tommy, you can play it...ain't but one string to note right there.' Well, I got to fooling with it, and it wasn't but a little bit till I started old 'Ruben.'"

This was a common tune in the Round Peak community, and both Charlie and Ben Jarrell fiddled it. Tommy said he learned most of the words from his uncle Dave Turney, his dad's half-brother. "He was a carpenter. He had to leave home before day every morning to walk to his work. And he'd go down that old ridge road about a half a mile from our house every day before morning a-singing that, and that's where I learned that song."

Tommy played the G slightly sharp of natural.

"Blowing the whistle":

54

You oughta been uptown
When old Ruben's train come down
You could hear the whistle blow a hundred miles

Old Ruben had a train
Run from England to Spain
But he couldn't get no letter from his home

If you don't believe I'm gone
Watch this train that I crawl on
Lord I'm nine hundred miles away from home

I'm nine hundred miles
Away from my wife and my child
Lord, I wish I was nine hundred more

If this train she runs right
We'll get home about daylight
Lord, I'm nine hundred miles away from home

Old Ruben went to town
And the police knocked him down
You could hear that boy holler a hundred miles

Old Ruben got killed
On that C&O line
And his poor body has never been found

They found his head
In the driver's wheel
About a mile and a half from town

Kenny Lowe's cabin, where Boggie Cockerham was raised, under restoration

Bauga "Boggie" Cockerham (1885-1967)

Boggie Cockerham, second cousin to the well-known Round Peak musician Fred Cockerham, showed Tommy how to play "Ruben" on banjo. He was also known for his rendition of "Darling Nellie Grey," which Kyle Creed (and possibly Tommy as well) learned from him. Boggie was known as one of the best banjo pickers in the Round Peak area, perhaps second only to Charlie Lowe. He was raised for the most part in the household of Kenny Lowe, himself a clawhammer banjo player born way back in 1833. Tona Hawks, aka Tony Lowe, the noted fiddler, was also taken in by this generous family, which produced several other excellent musicians as well. They were some of the Jarrells' nearest neighbors, living just over in the next hollow.

Kevin Donleavy interviewed Boyd McKinney, who gave this description of Boggie: "He didn't have much education. Kenny Lowe raised him. All he did in his young days was pick the banjo. Then he had a whole crowd of children, nine of 'em, all boys. Boggie didn't push himself on anybody. He wouldn't play the banjo much without you just insisted on it. Boggie was one of the best of the old-time banjo players. He knew Tommy Jarrell all his life. They played that old whanging style, pure old Round Peak stuff."

32. Shortening Bread

Tommy learned his unusual version of "Shortening Bread" from his father.

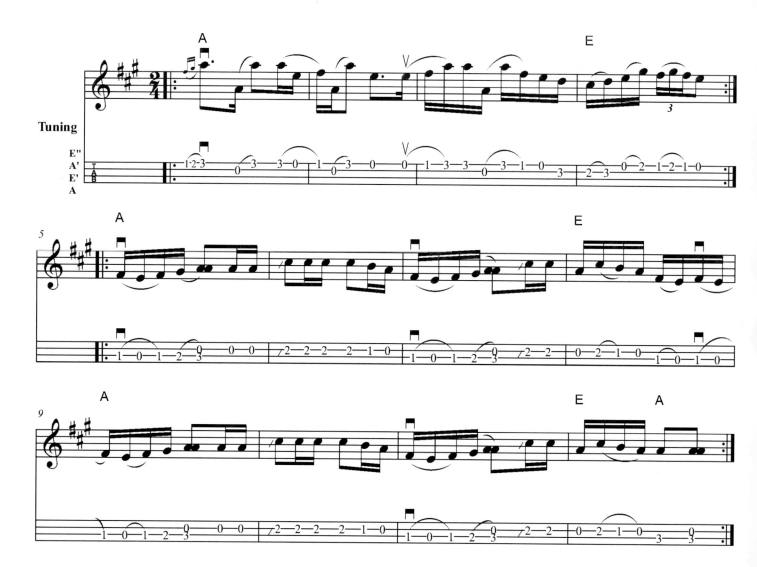

Cold hog's head, shortening bread
Gonna kill that baby, gonna kill him dead

Chorus:
My mama makes shortening, shortening
My mama makes shortening bread

Call for the doctor, the doctor said
Feed that baby on shortening bread

33. Sourwood Mountain

This is another tune from Ben and Charlie Jarrell. It has an interesting high part that's a little different than how the tune is usually played elsewhere.

Chickens crowing on the Sourwood Mountain
Hey, ho, tum-a-diddle-um-a-day
So many pretty gals that you can't count 'em
Hey, ho, tum-a-diddle-um-a-day

Big dog'll bark, little one'll bite you
Hey, ho, tum-a-diddle-um-a-day
Big gal'll kiss, little one'll fight you
Hey, ho, tum-a-diddle-um-a-day

34. Stay All Night

No title better captures the hospitality to which Tommy treated visitors, and he often quoted the first line of this song when he invited guests to stay overnight. The tune also turns up with a different high part in a recording by Fields Ward of Grayson County, Va., called "Way Down in North Carolina." It's also known as "Water Bound."

Stay all night and don't go home
Stay all night and don't go home
Stay all night and don't go home
Stay with me till morning

The river's up and I can't get across
The river's up and I can't get across
The river's up and I can't get across
Stay with me till morning

I give five dollars for an old blind horse
I give five dollars for an old blind horse
He sat down and I couldn't get across
Stay with me till morning

I kicked and I spurred, I couldn't get him in
I kicked and I spurred, I couldn't get him in
I give five dollars to take him back again
Stay with me till morning

Linda Higginbotham

Tommy Jarrell's home

The house at 734 S. Franklin Rd.

After he left Round Peak and had a family of his own, Tommy settled in the community of Toast on the outskirts of Mount Airy, N.C. During the years after his retirement and the death of his wife Nina, hundreds of visitors came to Tommy's house to make music with him or hear him play, and at his invitation many of them would "stay all night."

35. Sweet Sunny South

This was a popular song from the middle of the nineteenth century that entered into oral tradition. Though Charlie Poole's 1929 recording is better known, Ben Jarrell recorded the song in 1927 with the Southern Broadcasters. Ben didn't fiddle on the recording, but sang accompanied by two banjos.

Tommy played a neutral G, between natural and sharp.

Take me back to the place where I first saw the light
To the sweet sunny South take me home
Where the mockingbirds sang me to rest every night
Oh why was I tempted to roam?

I think with regret of the dear home I left
Of the warm hearth that sheltered me there
Of the wife and the dear ones of whom I'm bereft
For the old place again do I sigh

Take me back to the place where the orange trees bloom
To my spot in the evergreen shade
Where the flowers from the river's green margin they grow
They are sweet on the banks where we played

The path to our cottage they say has grown free
And the place is quite lonely around
And I know that the smiles and the forms I have seen
Now lie in the dark, mossy ground

Take me back, let me see what is left that I knew
Can it be that the old house is gone?
Dear friends of my childhood indeed must be few
And I must face death all alone

But yet I return to the place of my birth
Where the children have played round the door
Where they gather wild blossoms that grow round the path
They will echo our footsteps no more

Take me back to the place where my little ones sleep
Poor Mossa lies buried close by
And the graves of the loved ones I long there to meet
Among them to live till I die

36. The Tater Patch Tune

Tommy tells the story of how this tune originated about 1910 in Carroll County, Va. "A man named Ike Leonard made that tune. He was a-hoeing or plowing in his potato patch when it come to his mind. He quit whatever he was doing, went to the house and got his banjo, and played the tune till he knew he could remember it. That's how come they called it 'The Tater Patch Tune.'" Tommy played a neutral G.

Ike Leonard, the man who made "Tater Patch"

Isaac "Ike" Leonard (1884–1911)

Ike was a banjo picker who lived near Lambsburg in Carroll County, Va. It was known as a rough area, and indeed he lived only to the age of 27. In *Strings of Life* Kevin Donleavy presents evidence of an altercation between Ike and the family of a young woman he was seeing about 1906: a local man was sentenced to 60 days in jail and a fine of $250 on a charge of "maiming by shooting," and about the same time Ike and his brother Joe also were charged with "carrying concealed pistols." Kevin speculates that Ike sustained injuries in the shooting that ultimately proved fatal several years later. Although the pose suggests this is wedding photo, he did not wed the girl whose hand rests on his shoulder, but married a girl named Dollie Rippey instead. After she was widowed, Dollie married fiddler Logan Lowe, whose brother Charlie Barnett showed "Tater Patch" to Tommy Jarrell. According to Charlie's daughter Sel, Ike at one time had worked for her dad.

37. Train on the Island

Tommy's father played this tune and his mother used to sing it as well. It was widely played in Surry, Grayson, and Carroll counties. Tommy had forgotten all the verses he used to sing but one (the first one below), so I've included verses from other sources.

Train on the island, can't you hear it blow?
Go and tell that pretty little gal I ain't coming back no more
Go and tell that pretty little gal I ain't coming back no more

Train on the island, headed for the west
Go and tell that pretty little gal she's the one I love the best
Go and tell that pretty little gal she's the one I love the best

Train on the island, can't you hear it blow?
Go and tell that pretty little gal I'm sick and I can't go
Go and tell that pretty little gal I'm sick and I can't go

Train on the island, can't you hear it squeal?
Go and tell that pretty little gal how happy I do feel
Go and tell that pretty little gal how happy I do feel

38. When Sorrows Encompass Me Round

Tommy didn't profess to being particularly religious, but his rendition of "When Sorrows Encompass Me Round" could be deeply moving nonetheless. Tommy's words are from the Primitive Baptist songbook (the denomination to which he felt the greatest affinity), and the melody is essentially the same as the Sacred Harp hymn "Idumea." Tommy played the C and G notes of the scale slightly sharp of natural but not true sharps.

When sorrows encompass me round
And many distresses I see
Astonished, I cry, can a mortal be found
Surrounded with troubles like me?

Few seasons of peace I enjoy
And they are succeeded by pain
If ever few moments of praise I enjoy
I have hours and days to complain

Oh, when will my sorrows subside?
Oh, when will my suffering cease?
Oh, when to the bosom of Christ be conveyed
To the mansions of glory and bliss?

May I be prepared for that day
When Jesus shall bid me remove
That I may in rapture go shouting away
To the arms of my heavenly love

My spirit to Glory convey
My body laid low in the ground
I wish not a tear round my grave to be shed
But all join in praising around

No sorrows be vented that day
When Jesus has called me home
With singing and shouting let each brother say
"He's gone from all evil to come"

Immersed in the ocean of love
My soul like an angel shall sing
Till Christ shall descend with a shout from above
And make all creation to ring

Our bodies in dust shall obey
And swifter than thought shall arise
Then changed in a moment go shouting away
To the mansions of love in the sky

AE'A'C#'' tuning (key of A)

39. The Drunken Hiccups (Jack of Diamonds) 🎵

Houston Galyean of Low Gap was especially known in the area for fiddling "The Drunken Hiccups." Ben and Charlie Jarrell both learned it from him, and it was among the tunes Ben recorded for Gennett in 1927. Tommy learned it from his father, and it became one of his showpieces. The tune is played all over the South under many names.

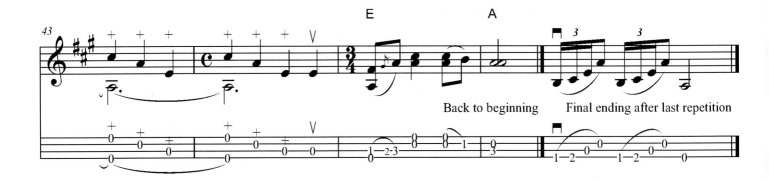

Tommy usually sang the chorus on the low part of the tune and the verse on the middle part, but occasionally he would sing a verse on the high part. You can sing it wherever it suits your voice. Tommy wasn't strict about playing the parts in the order presented here, and he didn't play the plucking part every time around. Sometimes for humorous effect he would hiccup to the plucking part.

I've played cards in England, I've gambled in Spain
Going back to Rhode Island, gonna play my last game

Chorus:
Jack of Diamonds, Jack of Diamonds, I know you from old
You've robbed my poor pockets of silver and gold

Get up in the morning, I stagger I reel
Doggone that corn whiskey, how bad I do feel*

Corn whiskey and pretty women, they've been my downfall
They've beat me and they've banged me, but I love them for all

My shoes is all tore up, my toes are sticking out
Don't get some corn whiskey, I'm a-going up the spout

I'll beat on the counter, I'll make the glass ring
More brandy, more brandy, more brandy to bring

Gonna drink, I'm a-gonna gamble, my money's my own
Them that don't like me can leave me alone

Gonna eat when I'm hungry, gonna drink when I'm dry
Get to feeling much better, I'm a-gonna sprout wings and fly

If the ocean was whiskey and I was a duck
I'd dive to the bottom and never come up

Now the ocean's not whiskey nor I ain't no duck
Just play the "Drunken Hiccups" and trust to my luck

I'll tune up my fiddle and rosin the bow
And make myself welcome wherever I go

* Ben Jarrell sang "God bless those pretty women, how happy I feel."

68

AD'A'E" tuning (key of D)

40. Arkansas Traveler

The music, plays, skits, and jokes associated with this tune appear to have originated in the middle of the 19th century, when they were performed to popular acclaim throughout the country. Vance Randolph gives credit to an Arkansan, Col. Sandford C. Faulkner, and his humorous accounts of his travels in Pope County, Arkansas, in the 1840s. First published in New York in 1850, the tune entered oral tradition and is one of the most common American fiddle tunes. Tommy played it as an instrumental, without singing or joke-telling.

69

41. Backstep Cindy (Stepback Cindy)

Ben Jarrell and his music partners Charlie and Tony Lowe overhauled "Old-Time Backstep Cindy" and came up with this. Tommy called it the "new" way of playing the tune, and felt it was a big improvement. The tunes were called "Backstep" or "Stepback" to distinguish them from the unrelated "Rockingham Cindy." It's hard to find chord changes in this tune; guitar players often stay on D throughout and punctuate it with bass runs.

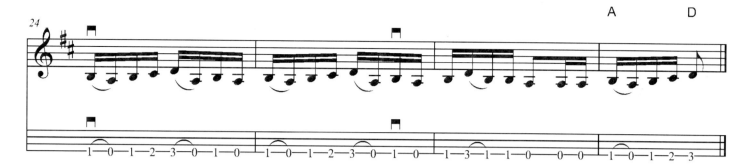

42. "Old-Time" Backstep Cindy (Holly Ding) 🔴disc

This is an old tune that Tommy described as having come from the "backside of the mountain" in Virginia. His father-in-law Charlie Barnett Lowe, among others, played the tune. Another name for it around Galax is "Holly Ding." The call-and-response structure suggests African American origins, and in fact in the book *Negro Folk Rhymes*, Thomas Tally presents a play song called "Holly Dink" that he collected in Tennessee.

71

43. The Bravest Cowboy

This song came to Round Peak about 1919. It was especially popular among young women, who sang it and played it on a "new" parlor instrument, the guitar. One of them was Tommy's sister Julie Jarrell Lyons. He once showed me a page on which she had written the words for him. Versions of the song have been collected mostly in the Ozarks and Texas, so it's interesting to see it crop up in the mountains of North Carolina.

I am the bravest cowboy that ever trod the West
I've been all over the Rockies, got bullets in my breast

In eighteen-hundred and sixty-three I joined the immigrant band
We marched from San Antonio, down by the Rio Grande

I saw the Indians coming, we heard them give their yell
My feelings at that moment no tongue could ever tell

I went out on the prairie, I learned to throw the line
I learned to pocket money, but I did not dress much fine

I rambled on back to Texas, where I learned to rob and steal
And when I robbed that cowboy, how happy I did feel

I wore a wide-brim white hat, my saddle too was fine
And when I courted a pretty girl, you bet I called her mine

I courted her for beauty, for love it was in vain
Till they carried me down to Dallas to wear a ball and chain

44. Cider (Stillhouse)

This tune is played in Surry County and across the state line in neighboring parts of Virginia as well; Matokie Slaughter of Pulaski played a particularly nice version of it on banjo. Tommy learned the tune from his father.

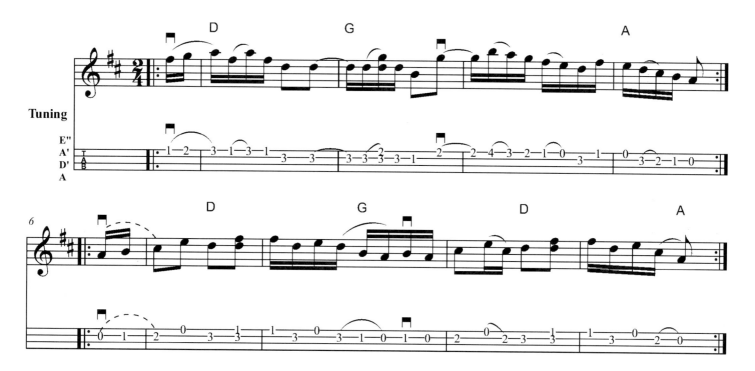

You be the horse and I'll be the rider
We'll go down to the stillhouse to get a little cider

Cider, cider, a little more cider
Down to the stillhouse to get a little cider

Hickory horse and a white oak saddle
And a pretty little girl riding astraddle

Cider, cider, a little more cider
Cider, cider, a little more cider

45. Ducks on the Mill Pond

Ben and Charlie Jarrell both knew this piece, a courting-themed tune that goes way back in the Round Peak area. It was played across the mountain as well, although you can hear distinct differences between Tommy Jarrell's Round Peak style of playing it and that of, say, noted Galax fiddler Emmett Lundy.

Ducks on the mill pond, geese in the clover
Tell them pretty gals to come on over

Ducks on the mill pond, geese in the ocean
All them pretty gals just in the notion

Rain come wet me, sun come dry me
Stand back pretty gals, don't you come a-nigh me

All I want in God's creation's
A pretty little wife and a big plantation

74

The old Freeman place

Tell them pretty gals to come on over

Banjo player Dix "Dick" Freeman (1908–1996) lived in this house on Richards Road in Round Peak. It was the site of many dances down through the years and is still owned by his daughter and son-in-law, Polly and Chester McMillian.

46. Fall on My Knees

Round Peak musicians called this "Lonesome Road" until another tune, "Lonesome Road Blues," became popular. It's known by a number of other names as well. Bertie Mae Dickens of Ennice, N.C., called it "County Jail."

76

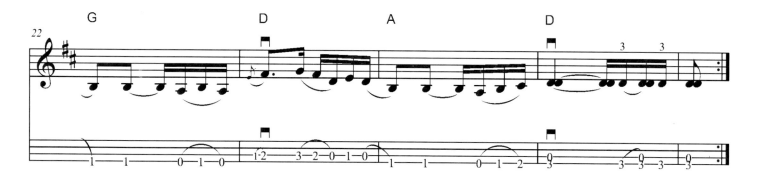

Oh, I fall on my knees, and I pray to thee
To come and stand around with me, little girl
Stand around with me

Look up, look down that lonesome old road
And it's hang down your little head and cry, little girl
Hang down your little head and cry

There's more than one, Lord, there's more than two
No other little woman like you,* little girl
No other little woman like you

I wish to the Lord that I'd never been born
Or died when I was young, little girl
Died when I was young

I never would have kissed your red, rosy cheeks
Or heard your lying tongue, little girl
Heard your lying tongue

You told me one, you told me two
You told me ten thousand lies, little girl
You told me ten thousand lies

You told me more lies than the stars in the sky
And you'll never get to heaven when you die, little girl
You'll never get to heaven when you die

My suitcase is packed and my trunk it's done gone
It's goodbye, little woman, I'm gone, gone
Goodbye, little woman, I'm gone

* Sometimes Tommy sang "Ten thousand little girls, but none like you"

47. Fisher's Hornpipe

Older fiddlers in the Galax area commonly played "Fisher's Hornpipe" in the key of G, but Tommy and other Round Peak fiddlers played it in D. Tommy told Barry Poss about one night when he and his dad were visiting Logan Lowe: Tommy played this tune, and Ben said "By God, that's the best I ever heard 'Fisher's Hornpipe' played." It was the only time he could remember his dad praising his fiddling.

48. Forky Deer

This very old and widespread tune came to Round Peak from Carroll County, Va., where Tommy heard his father-in-law, Charlie Barnett Lowe, play it on banjo with fiddlers John Rector and Fred Hawks. "Forky Deer" was among several tunes John recorded for the Library of Congress in 1937 with his band, the Wildcats.

49. Fortune

This is a very common tune in this part of North Carolina and adjacent parts of Virginia, and has apparently been around for a long time. Tommy learned it from his father.

Once I had a fortune
All locked up in my trunk
I lost it all a-gambling*
One night when I got drunk

Wish I had a pretty little horse
Corn to feed him on
And a pretty little wife to stay at home
And feed him when I'm gone

* Sometimes "…in a poker game"

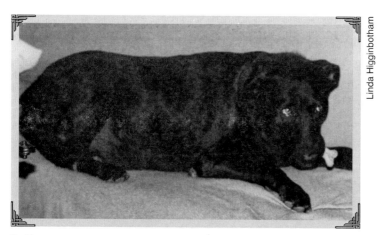

Linda Higginbotham

Bolivar

Tommy Jarrell's dog

Tommy named his black Labrador retriever after Simón Bolívar, the Great Liberator of South America (although he pronounced it "BAWL-i-ver"). An enormous, good-natured bear of a dog, Bolivar usually claimed the best seat in the house (the couch) and carried a milk bone in his mouth until he had enough room in his belly to swallow it—whereupon Tommy would give him another one to carry around.

After Tommy's death, Andy Cahan adopted Bolivar. I remember one day we were playing music with Andy at his house in Galax. In the middle of the first tune we heard a commotion, and Bolivar rushed in—apparently in hopes of finding Tommy.

50. The Joke on the Puppy (Rye Straw)

Ben Jarrell got this tune from Civil War veteran Pet McKinney. Tommy learned it listening to Ben's music sessions with Charlie Lowe. The song is known for its humorous scatological verses—so much so that Tommy was careful about even fiddling the tune in mixed company unless he knew them well, much less singing any verses. I've cleaned up a couple of verses (top of the opposite page) to make them suitable for general audiences.

Dog ate a rye straw, dog ate a minner [minnow]
Dog ate a catfish big enough for dinner

Dog ate a rye straw, dog ate a nettle
Dog ate a rye straw, sharp as any needle

51. Mississippi Sawyer

This is one of the most common and widespread American fiddle tunes. Tommy's way of playing it is perfectly straightforward; but for such an apparently ordinary tune there are a surprising number of "crooked" versions played by older musicians.

52. New River Train

The Chesapeake & Ohio Railroad completed a section of track along the New River in 1873. Ironically one of the world's oldest rivers, the New River flows through Grayson and Carroll counties in Virginia (where the tune was especially popular) on its way to the Kanawha River in south central West Virginia. Tommy got the tune from his father, and picked up verses from different people. Mike Seeger quotes him: "I've heard it sung plum on up to the eleventh verse...something about 'heaven' to wind up. I don't sing it that far no more."

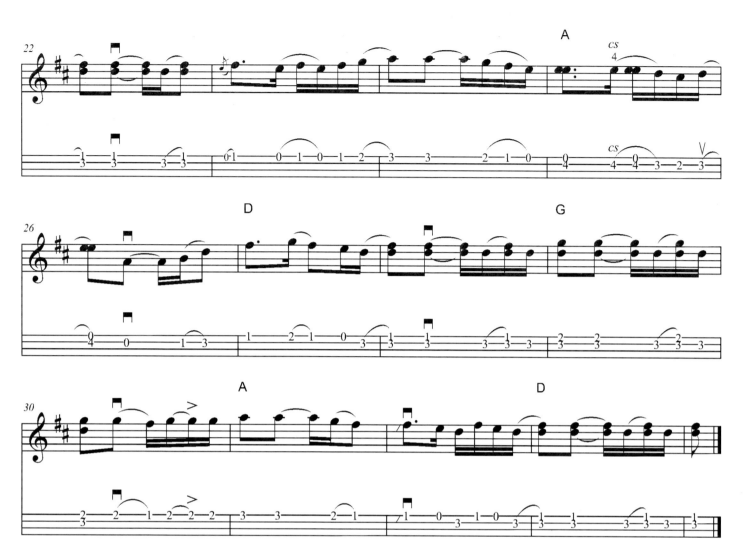

Oh, it's darling, you can't love just one
Darling, you can't love just one
You can't love just one and have any fun
Lord it's darling, you can't love just one

Chorus:
I'm riding on that New River train
Riding on that New River train
Same old train that brought me here
Gonna carry me away again

Oh, it's darling, you can't love two
Darling, you can't love two
You can't love two and your little heart be true
Darling, you can't love two

Oh, it's darling, you can't love three
Darling, you can't love three
You can't love three and then love me
Darling, you can't love three

Oh, it's darling, you can't love four
Darling, you can't love four
You can't love four and love me any more
Darling, you can't love four

Oh, it's darling, you can't love five
Darling, you can't love five
You can't love five and then be my wife
Darling, you can't love five

Oh, it's darling, you can't love six
Darling, you can't love six
You can't love six or you'll be in a hell of a fix
Darling, you can't love six

Oh, it's darling, you can't love seven
Darling, you can't love seven
You can't love seven and still get to heaven
Darling, you can't love seven

Oh, it's darling, you can't love eight
Darling, you can't love eight
You can't love eight and meet me at the pearly gate
Darling, you can't love eight

53. Old Jimmy Sutton

Tommy was a natural-born entertainer. He would throw himself into this tune, arms flapping, body weaving, both feet keeping time, bleating like a lamb in distress.

Sheep, sheep, sheep and mutton
If you can't dance that, you can't dance nothin'
And a baah!
Baah! Old Jimmy Sutton

We'll kill us a sheep and eat the mutton
And save the tail for old Jimmy Sutton
And a baah!
Baah! Old Jimmy Sutton

54. Old Molly Hare

This is one of those very old tunes with roots in the British Isles, where its several titles include "The Fairy Dance." Tommy rendered this simple melody with surprisingly complex bowing.

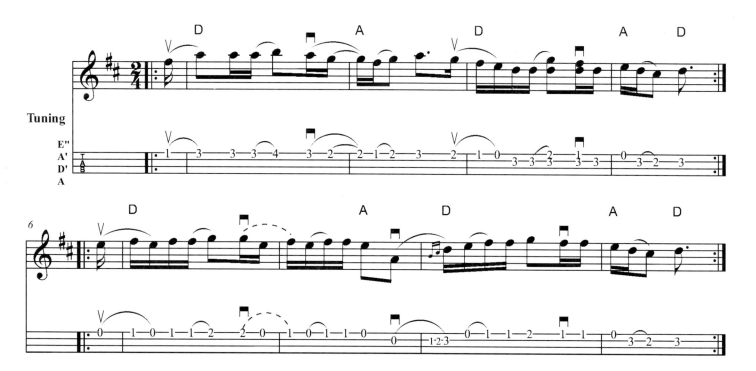

Old Molly Hare, what'ya doing there?
Sitting on the hillside, shooting at a bear

Old Molly Hare, what'ya doing there?
Running through the cotton patch as hard as I can tear

Old Molly Hare, what'ya doing there?
Sitting by the butter dish a-picking out a hair

55. Peek-a-Boo (Green Gravel)

"School breakings" on the last day of the school year were important events in mountain communities, with much ceremony and festivity, including food, games, student speeches, and music. The children would line up and march, led by prominent citizens and musicians. Tommy described breakings at Round Peak's Ivy Green School where two lines of children were led by Tommy's grandfather Rufus Jarrell and "old man" Pet McKinney (probably by virtue of their status as Civil War veterans), with music provided by fiddlers Ben Jarrell and Tony Lowe. This ancient and widespread tune was a popular marching number at such events. Also known as "Green Gravel," "Jackson's March," "Chapel Hill Serenade," and "Green Willis," among other names, it is linked according to some sources to a traditional English tune called "New Rigged Ship." It bears no relationship to the "Peek-a-Boo Waltz" commonly played in other parts of the country.

Tommy remembered only a couple of fragments of verses:

Peek-a-boo, peek-a-boo, you rascal you
I see you hiding behind that tree

Green gravel, green gravel, the grass is so green
As beauteous beauty as ever I've seen

56. Polly Put the Kettle On

Round Peak musicians played this as a three-part tune; elsewhere it usually has only two. Tommy gave Charlie Lowe credit for adding the third part. Charlie also collaborated in adding third parts to "Backstep Cindy," and "John Brown's Dream."

Polly put the kettle on
Jenny blow the dinner horn
Polly put the kettle on
We'll all take tea

57. Richmond Cotillion

"Richmond Cotillion" was among the tunes Ben Jarrell recorded with DaCosta Woltz's Southern Broadcasters in 1927 for the Gennett label. As with "John Brown's Dream," the recording showcased Ben's ability to call a dance while he fiddled.

58. Ricketts' Hornpipe

In much of the southern Appalachians, hornpipes survive only in name; and in Round Peak, only in two or three tune names at that. Tommy used the word mainly to describe a slower-paced, ornate fiddle style of which he wasn't particularly fond—such as some of the old Galax fiddlers played—and especially to contrast that with the style of fiddling popular in Round Peak. Many of the twists and turns of "Ricketts' Hornpipe" as published in standard tunebooks are streamlined in Tommy's version, particularly in the coarse part of the tune.

59. Rochester Schottische (Walking in the Parlor)

Ben Jarrell called this tune "Rochester Schottische," but Charlie Lowe and others called it "Walking in the Par-lor." Apparently unrelated to the family of tunes usually called "Rochester Schottische" *or* the family of tunes usually called "Walking in the Parlor," this mysterious piece isn't even a schottische.

60. Rockingham Cindy

This is the same tune that's simply called "Cindy" elsewhere in the mountains. Round Peakers called it "Rockingham Cindy" to distinguish it from the unrelated "Backstep Cindy." There's an interesting shift in timing between the fine and coarse parts of this tune (and vice versa): it feels crooked, but in fact there are no missing or added beats, and it will feel perfectly natural once you get used to it. That quirk of timing is pretty much standard for this tune among older musicians throughout the southern Appalachians, and is not peculiar to Round Peak.

Never loved old Cindy, don't expect I ever shall
Never loved old Cindy, but I love old Cindy's gal

Chorus:
It's come on home, Cindy, Cindy
Come on home,* Cindy, Cindy

Where'd you get your whiskey, where'd you get your dram?
Where'd you get your whiskey at? Way down in Rockingham

Where'd you get your whiskey, where'd you get your dram?
Where'd you get your whiskey at? [spoken:] Well it don't make a damn…

* Sometimes: "Knock along home"

Tommy and Brad, 1984

Where'd you get your whiskey?

Tommy wouldn't reveal his source, but as a former moonshiner himself, he knew where to get high-quality white liquor, kept it on hand, and was generous in sharing it. When he ran out, second choice was I.W. Harper 100 proof, which he got at the state store in Dobson, N.C.

61. Sally Ann

Tommy said his father and Tony Lowe "jazzed up" the old-time "Sally Ann" to make this new one. However, he also said, "I learned that [third part] from Hiram Moody in Lambsburg, and I brought it down to North Carolina and showed everybody else." Hiram is said to have learned the tune from Tony Lowe, so it would appear that Ben and Tony overhauled the first two parts and Hiram added the third. In any case, the new three-part version became so popular that resident Chester McMillian jokingly calls it the "Round Peak National Anthem."

Sung at random on the second part:
Ride the buggy, yes I am
Ride in the buggy, Sally Ann
Sally Ann, Sally Ann

I'm going to the wedding, yes I am
I'm a-going to the wedding, old Sally Ann

Greenback dollar
Greenback dollar, good as gold

Pass the brandy,
Pass the brandy, Sally Ann

Sift your meal and save the bran
The old cow needs it, Sally Ann

Sally's in the garden sifting sand
Susan's in the bed with the hogeye man
I'm going home with Sally Ann
I'm going home with Sally Ann

Hiram's verses, sung at random on the third part:
How in the world can I swing Susan?
Susan's done and gone
She's done and gone
Susan's gone away

Who in the world in the doggone nation's
Throwing them rocks at me?*
All of them rocks, all them rocks
All of them rocks at me

* Lambsburg was a rough area. Young men sometimes hid near the road and threw rocks at passersby.

62. "Old-Time" Sally Ann

Tommy called this "old-time Sally Ann" to distinguish it from the new version. He said the older tune came from up the mountain in Virginia. There are actually several subtly different versions of the tune from nearby communities in Virginia; this is probably the way his father-in-law, Charlie Barnett Lowe, played it.

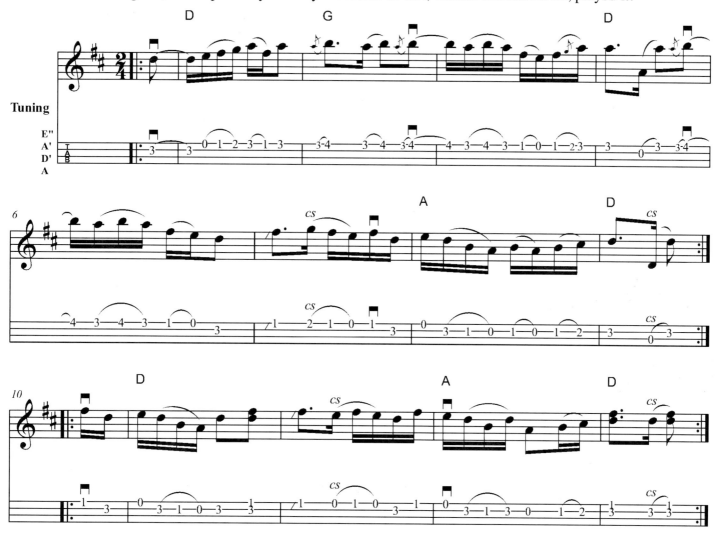

Did you ever see a muskrat, Sally Ann
Dragging his slick tail through the sand?

63. Say, Darling, Say

This is the old mockingbird lullabye made into a fiddle tune. "My mother sang that when I was a little boy," said Tommy, "but she didn't have that verse about the chitlin strut. I put that to it." He said a chitlin strut was a dance held by black folks in the fall, when they slaughtered their hogs. "You can play that," he encouraged me, "there ain't nothin' to it." Actually, there's quite a bit to it: in much of the tune, the groupings of three sixteenth notes or the equivalent makes the bowing almost polyrhythmic!

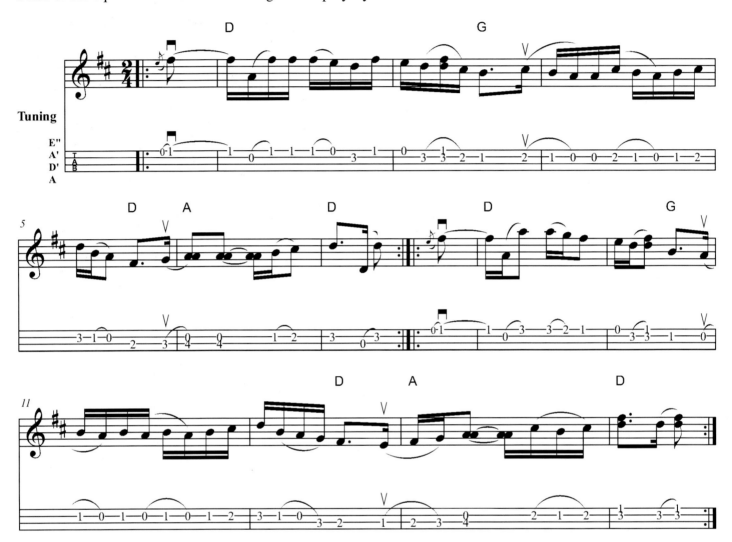

Hush up, darling, don't say a word
Daddy's gonna buy you a mockingbird
Say, darling, say

If that mockingbird don't sing
Daddy's gonna buy you a diamond ring
Say, darling, say

If that diamond ring turns to brass
Daddy's gonna buy you a looking glass
Say, darling, say

If that looking glass gets broke
Daddy's gonna buy you a billy goat
Say, darling, say

If that billy goat don't butt
Daddy's gonna do the chitlin strut
Say, darling, say

Oh, little darling, if you was mine
You wouldn't do nothing but starch and iron
Say, darling, say

Starch and iron would be your trade
And I'd get drunk and lay in the shade
Say, darling, say

The Jarrells in 1901. Susie Amburn is seated by her husband, Ben Jarrell; Charlie Jarrell is behind them with a fiddle.

Susie Amburn Jarrell (1882–1961)

The wife of Ben Jarrell and mother of Tommy Jarrell, Susie Amburn is pictured above in a badly damaged photograph from 1901. If you look closely, you can see the infant Tommy on her lap. Tommy remembers her singing such songs as "Say, Darling, Say," "The Blackest Crow," and "Train on the Island."

64. Soldier's Joy (Love Somebody)

One of the classic fiddle tunes in both the U.S. and the Old World, "Soldier's Joy" has been played around Round Peak as long as anyone can remember. It was also known locally as "Love Somebody." Tommy developed his signature bow-rocking variation on the low part by following the banjo playing of his father-in-law: "I used to play that with Charlie Barnett Lowe; sometimes he'd just get to rolling, up there on the bass string."

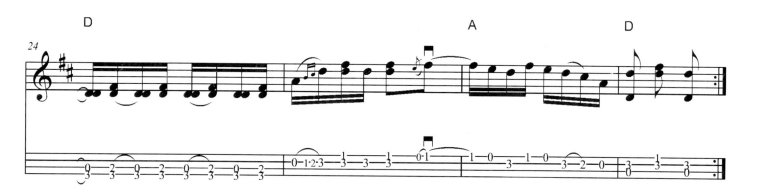

I love somebody, yes I do
I love somebody, yes I do
I love somebody, yes I do
And I bet you five dollars that you can't guess who

I'm gonna get a drink, don't you want to go?
I'm gonna get a drink, don't you want to go?
I'm gonna get a drink, don't you want to go?
Hold on, soldier's joy

Grasshopper sitting on a sweet tater vine
Grasshopper sitting on a sweet tater vine
Grasshopper sitting on a sweet tater vine
Along come a chicken, says you are mine

Twenty-five cents for the morphine
Fifteen cents for the beer
Twenty-five cents for the morphine
Gonna carry me away from here

65. Sugar Hill

Kevin Donleavy notes that a hill near Lambsburg, Va., known by locals as Sugar Hill, concealed a number of moonshine stills and had the reputation for being a rough and dangerous area. Toenail Gap is nearby, a steep gap in the Blue Ridge that was once used by Carroll County residents to take wheelbarrow loads of tanbark to market in Mount Airy. As in the song, Tommy used to go up Toenail Gap to visit his gal, Charlie Barnett Lowe's daughter Nina. Said Tommy, "you couldn't hardly walk up there, much less roll a wheelbarrow."

Five cents in my pocket change
Two dollars in my bill
If I had ten dollars more
I'd climb old Sugar Hill

Jaybird and the sparrowhawk
They had a little fight together
They fought all around the briarpatch
And they never jerked a feather

If I had no horse to ride
I'd be found a-walking
Up and down old Toenail Gap
To hear that gal a-talking

102

Charlie Barnett with one of his beloved hunting dogs

Charlie Barnett Lowe (1872–1924)

Tommy's father-in-law, usually called Charlie Barnett to distinguish him from Charlie Lowe of Round Peak, was the brother of fiddler Logan Lowe and a respected banjo picker in his own right. He was a friend of Tommy's family, loved his hunting dogs, and enjoyed fox hunting with Ben Jarrell's half-brother Dave Turney. Charlie lived across the mountain, on the other side of Toenail Gap in Carroll County, Va., with his wife Ardena and three daughters.

Tommy spent some time in Virginia after a fight with his uncle in 1920. At Charlie's invitation, Tommy stayed with the family off and on for the next few years making liquor, helping with the crops, courting Charlie's daughter Nina, and of course playing a lot of music. Charlie introduced Tommy to a number of musicians in Carroll County, including John Rector and Fred Hawks. Tommy learned "Let Me Fall" and the "Tater Patch" tune from Charlie, as well as his distinctive low variation on "Soldiers' Joy." Tommy and Nina married in 1923; her mother, Ardena, after whom they named their only daughter, died in September 1924; and Charlie himself died just three months later, on Christmas morning.

66. Susananna Gal

Also known as "Western Country," this is a common tune in southwest Virginia and northwest North Carolina. The horses named in the song are a reference to two uncles of Tommy's wife, Logan and Morgan Lowe. Tommy played a lot of music with Logan, a fiddler known for his sense of humor, who doubtless enjoyed the joke.

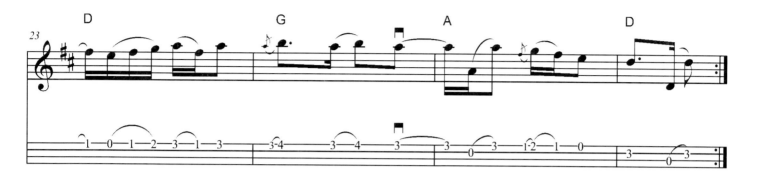

How do you make your living now, Susananna?
How do you make your living now, Susananna gal?

Rock into a notion now, Susananna
Rock into a notion now, Susananna gal

I'll hitch old Logan in the lead and Morgan in behind
I'm going down that rocky road, gonna see that gal of mine

I'm going to the western country now, Susananna
I'm going to the western country now, Susananna gal

Sixteen horses in my team as I go riding by
If I don't get to old Susananna, Lord, I'll know the reason why

Can't stay here if you can't shuck corn, Susananna
Can't stay here if you can't shuck corn, Susananna gal

How do you make your living now, Susananna?
Drinking whiskey and playing cards, Susananna gal

105

67. Tempie

Fred Cockerham's father-in-law, Houston Galyean, played this tune. Since Houston's wife was named Tempie, Fred speculated that the tune originally came from Houston. But the basic outline and structure of the melody appear to be very old, and versions of it are played widely throughout the South under a variety of names.

Tempie, roll down your bangs
Tempie, roll down your bangs
Roll down your bangs
And see how they hang
It's Tempie, roll down your bangs

I wish I was a mole in the ground
I wish I was a mole in the ground
If I was a mole in the ground
I'd root these mountains down
Lord, I wish I was a mole in the ground

Tempie, what am I gonna do?
Tempie, what am I gonna do?
My land debts are due
And my whiskey bill, too
It's Tempie what am I gonna do?

I wish I was a lizard in the spring
I wish I was a lizard in the spring
If I was a lizard in the spring
I could hear old Tempie sing
Oh, I wish I was a lizard in the spring

68. They Say It Is Sinful to Flirt (Willie My Darling)

This ballad crops up in the repertoires of many musicians in the Grayson, Carroll, and Surry county area, including Kyle Creed, Fred Cockerham, Ernest Stoneman, and Wade Ward. The words here are from my father, Dick Leftwich, who got the song from his uncle George Leftwich, originally from Fancy Gap, Va.

See next page for lyrics

They Say It Is Sinful to Flirt (Willie My Darling)

(Transcription on previous page)

Oh they say it is sinful to flirt
And they tell me my heart's made of stone
And they tell me to speak to him kind
Or else leave the poor boy alone

They say he is only a boy
But I'm sure he's much older than me
And if they would but leave us alone
I am sure we much happier would be

I remember one night what he said
That he loved me for more than his life
And he called me his darling, his pet
And asked me to be his darling wife

"Oh Willie," I said with a sigh
"I'm afraid I will have to say no"
And he took the white rose from my hair
And said, "Goodbye darling, I must go"

Next morning poor Willie was dead
He was drowned in the pool by the mill
And the cold, crystal waters flowed o'er him
As they ran along down the hill

His body so cold I beheld
His blue eyes and his face looked so fair
And next to his pale lips he held
The white rose that I wore in my hair

Oh Willie, my darling, come back
I will always be faithful to you
Oh Willie, my darling, come back
I will always be faithful to you

69. The Wreck of the Old 97

Tommy's words seem to be an adaptation of the older "Ship that Never Returned" on which the tune is based, rather than the usual set of lyrics popularized through commercial recordings.

It was on one cold and frosty morning
Smoke rolled from a long smokestack
Ninety-seven pulled out from old Louisville, Kentucky
With a crew that never come back

Just one more trip, said the sleepy old conductor
As he kissed his loving wife
I've stolen enough money
    from the Norfolk & Western company
To maintain us the rest of our lives

But she never returned, no she never returned
And her fate is yet unlearned
[remainder of verse played instrumentally]

Just one more trip, said the sleepy old miner
As he staggered out of bed
The freight train is coming and we'll all get our money
And we'll paint this old town red

109

70. The Yellow Rose of Texas

Said Tommy of his father, "He liked that 'Yellow Rose of Texas.' He hardly ever picked up a fiddle what he didn't play that tune." It was another of the pieces that Ben recorded with DaCosta Woltz's Southern Broadcasters.

The yellow rose of Texas I'm going back to see
There ain't no other cowboy* knows her but me

She's the sweetest rose of color this cowboy ever knew
Her eyes are bright like diamonds and sparkle like the dew

She cried so when I left her, it like to broke my heart
And if I ever see her, we never more shall part

I'm going back to Texas, I'm now on my way
When I get back to Texas, in Texas I'll stay

When I get back to Austin, how happy I will be
With the yellow rose of Texas a-sitting on my knee

* I've changed this from the original "darkie" to suit modern sensibilities.

DD'A'D" tuning (key of D)

71. Boll Weevil 🎵💿

A plantation show came to the fair at Mount Airy in 1922 or '23, where Tommy heard this song performed by a singer he described as a "yellow gal": a light-skinned black woman, very tall, accompanying herself with just a tambourine. Tommy went to see the show twice just so he could learn the song. He told Ray Alden, "Now you talk about a woman that could sing; now her voice would tremble and just go way on up yonder, cause the hair to nearly rise up on your head." Tommy made it into a fiddle tune, with a neutral C and sliding notes preserving the bluesy character of the original.

Boll weevil told the farmer
You better treat me right
I'll eat up all your cotton
Sleep in your granary tonight

Boll weevil told the farmer
You need no Ford machine
I'll eat up all your cotton
Can't buy no gasoline

Don't see no water
But I'm about to drown
I can't see no fire
But I'm a-burning down

I seen a spider
Running up and down the wall
He must have been a-going
To get his ashes hauled

111

72. Bonaparte's Retreat

Tommy learned this one from his wife's uncle Logan Lowe, who lived near Lambsburg, Va. "We'd danced over at his house one night, just about all night, and laid down and slept a little bit. And he got up the next morning, and he got the fiddle and he tuned it like this [DDAD]. He said 'I'm going to play General Washington's tune for you this morning.' And he sat down, and here's what he played. Called it 'Bonaparte's Retreat.'" Logan had learned the tune from his neighbor, the noted fiddler Zach Payne, who was a Confederate veteran of the Civil War. When Tommy would play the tune, he'd usually speed up at the end of the last time through to represent Bonaparte quickening the pace of his retreat.

73. Ryland Spencer

Tommy learned this song after 1920, when the Jarrells moved to the outskirts of Mount Airy. Although Tommy called it "Ryland Spencer," Kevin Donleavy suggests it might have orginally been "Rawley and Spencer," the names of two black families in Mount Airy. Tommy in fact got the song from one Jim Rawley: "He'd come down the road by home every Sunday morning, a-picking the guitar right soft, he didn't want to wake nobody up. But I slept upstairs, right on the side of the road, and I'd hear him come by singing that song. My brother-in-law [Jim Gardner] learned it from him, and I learned it from my brother-in-law." Fields Ward, a musician from Grayson County, Va., also sang a nice version, which he called "Riley and Spencer." Paul Brown tells me that Fields learned the song from black railroad workers.

Oh, Ryland Spencer's done gone dry
Lord, there ain't no whiskey in this town
No, there ain't no whiskey in this town

I can eat more chicken than a pretty girl can fry
Lord, I'll tell more of them doggone lies
Yes, I can tell more of them doggone lies

You can tromp down the flowers all around my grave
But they'll rise and bloom again
Yes, they'll rise and bloom again

I can eat more fat meat than you can cook in a week
Lord, I'll tell more of them doggone lies
Yes, I'll tell more of them doggone lies

Courtesy Jessie Rawley

Jim Rawley (1900–1982)

Pictured here with his wife Jesse on their 60th anniversary, Jim Rawley was the singer/guitarist from whom Tommy and his brother-in-law learned "Ryland Spencer." He was a WPA worker and the son of banjo player Charlie Rawley.

AD'A'D" tuning (key of D)

74. Frankie Baker (Frankie and Albert) 🎵

This song was popular in the mountains early in the 20th century. According to some sources, it's based on events that took place in St. Louis in October of 1899. Frankie was a 22-year-old dancer who shot her 17-year old lover Allen Britt (which the folk process turned into "Albert") over his affair with Alice Pryor ("Alice Fry"). Frankie claimed self-defense and was acquitted. She died in 1950 in a mental institution.

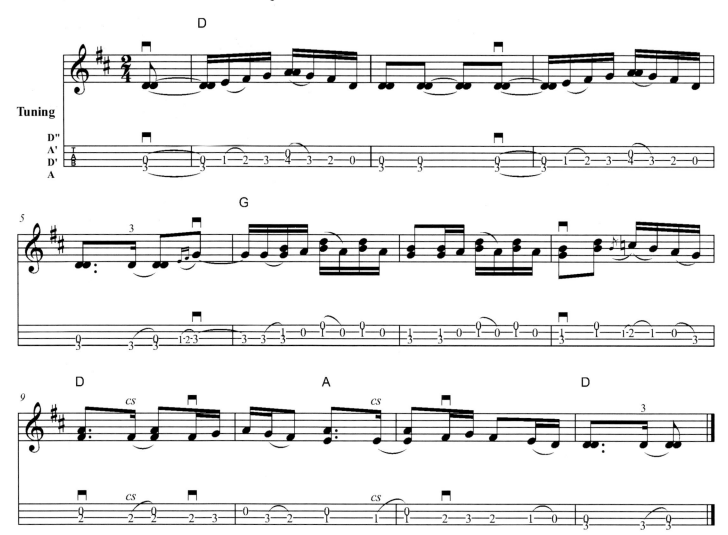

Frankie Baker was a good gal	"Come here to me little Albert, 'cause I don't mean no fun
It's everybody knows	If you don't come and go with the one you love
She paid a hundred dollars for a suit of Albert's clothes	I'll shoot you with your own gun
Because she loved her old man so	You've done me wrong, you've done me wrong"
Frankie went down to the barroom	He went all around the table, he got down on his knees
She called for a glass of beer	Crying out, "Please darling wife,
She said to the bartender, "Is my loving Albert in here?	Don't shoot me Frankie, please
He's my man, my gambling man."	I've done you wrong, I've done you wrong"
The barroom tender says "Frankie,	He crawled all around the table and he got up off of the floor
Girl I cannot lie	Bang, bang, bang went Frankie's gun
He just left here a moment ago with a girl named Alice Fry	She shot him with a forty-four
He's your man, but he's doing you wrong"	She killed her man, her gambling man
Frankie looked over the transom	Frankie had two little children, a boy and a girl
She saw to her surprise	If ever they see their father's face
There stood her gambling man making love to Alice Fry	They'll see it in another world
"You're my man, my gambling man"	She killed her man, her gambling man

114

75. Tumblin Gap (Cumberland Gap)

This is the Round Peak version of one of the most widely played Southern fiddle tunes, "Cumberland Gap." Tommy said it first came to Round Peak about 1915. The name isn't as different as it looks; local dialect tends to compress words in such a way that Cumberland is actually pronounced "Cumblin." Somewhere along the line a T replaced the initial C.

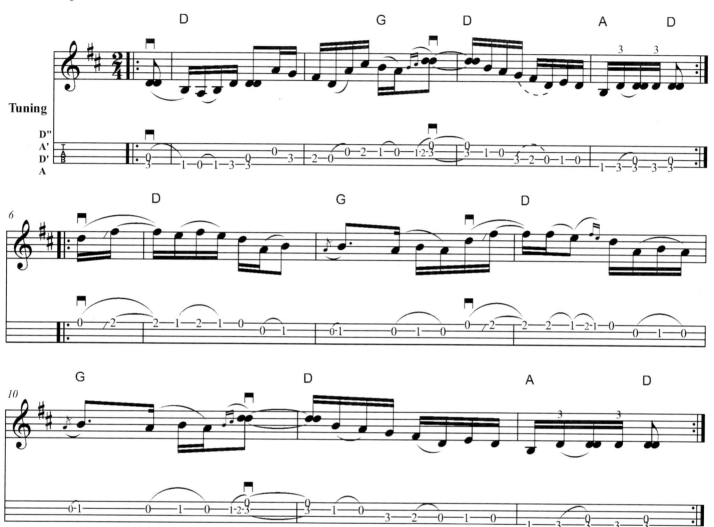

I'm going back to Tumblin Gap
To see my granny and my grandpap

I'll save my money and I'll buy me a farm
And raise sweet taters as long as your arm
Long as your arm, long as your arm
I'll raise sweet taters as long as your arm

Old Aunt Kate, old Aunt Sal
Old maid's sure got a pretty little gal
Pretty little gal, pretty little gal
Old maid's sure got a pretty little gal

Old Aunt Kate, if you don't care
Leave my demijohn sitting right there
If it ain't there when I get back
I'll raise sand* in the Tumblin Gap

I'll lay down and take a little nap
Wake up sober in the Tumblin Gap
Tumblin Gap, Tumblin Gap
Wake up sober in the Tumblin Gap

Now when I die, don't bury me at all
Just pickle my bones in alcohol
Lay my hands on top of my chest
And tell them pretty gals I've gone to rest

* Depending on his audience, sometimes Tommy sang "hell."

115

GD'A'D" tuning (key of G)

76. Flatwoods 🎵

Civil War veteran Zach Payne was a fiddler of renown who lived near Lambsburg, Va. His reluctance to play was well known. Tommy told how he went to visit Zach about 1920: "Oh, he said he never fooled with it no more. When we told his wife who we was she said, 'Zach, you get your fiddle and play these boys a tune. I've danced to many a reel at their granddaddy's.' Well, he went and got it. It had a piece of copper over the fingerboard. Where he'd been a-noting the strings it looked shiny as a new penny, and it told on him. I said, 'I can see you don't never play none.'" Zach grinned and finally played the tunes Tommy requested, "Billy in the Low Ground" and "Leather Britches," then he played two more: "Devil in the Strawstack" and "Flatwoods." Tommy kept the last two in his head till he got home and worked them out on his fiddle. He never learned the others.

GD'A'E" tuning (various keys)

77. Cackling Hen

Tommy played this for me on my first visit. It's a straightforward take this old, widespread tune. Every old fiddler in the South seems to play some version of this; some are very showy, with elaborate chicken imitations.

78. Dance All Night with a Bottle in Your Hand 💿

The first time I asked Tommy about this tune, he had some trouble remembering how it went. He said he hadn't played it in a long time. A 1924 mishap in a Ford Roadster took part of Tommy's left thumb, and he complained that made it difficult for him to slide back down after hitting the high note in the fine part of the tune. "I always make a mess of it," he said, although he actually played it quite well. Wade Ward of Grayson County, Va., had a very similar version.

79. Devil in the Strawstack

Tommy learned this old tune along with "Flatwoods" on his visit to Civil War veteran Zach Payne (see the introduction to "Flatwoods," p. 106). As in so many of his modal tunes, here again Tommy used a neutral G note.

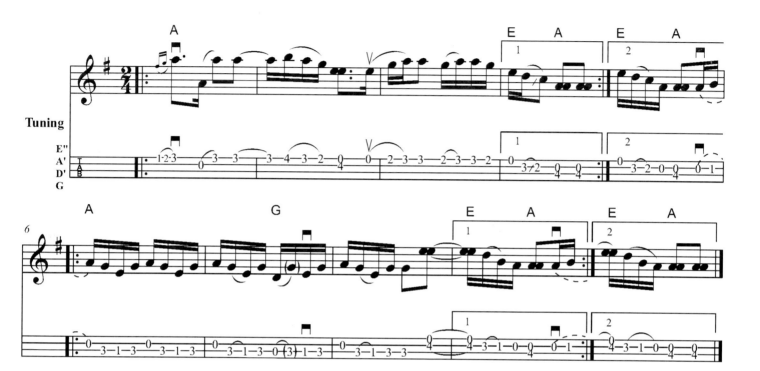

Never seen the like since I've been born
Devil in the strawstack, sticking out his horn

80. Old Buck (Paddy on the Turnpike) 🔘

Tommy said, "I was trying to learn 'Paddy on the Turnpike' and that's what I come up with. Rafe Brady [a noted fiddler from Carroll County, Va.] was down here, and I got him to play "Paddy on the Turnpike" for me, oh, two or three times. That's back when he was making music with my brothers Early and Oscar, along about nineteen and forty-two. Well, he come back in about six months, and I was playing that there. He says, 'Tommy, that ain't "Paddy on the Turnpike," that's "Old Buck."' Now whether they's a tune named 'Old Buck' or not, I don't know, but that's what he said. I don't know if he was just carrying on or not, but that's what I've always called it ever since."

120

81. Piney Woods Gal

Frank Jenkins (1888-1945), a well-known musician from the vicinity of Dobson, N.C., was in DaCosta Woltz's Southern Broadcasters along with Ben Jarrell. Tommy learned "Piney Woods Gal" from Frank about 1926. Tommy believed this was the original from which "Sally Johnson" and "Katy Hill" were made. Referring to commercial recordings of those tunes, Tommy said "They took it down to Nashville and adulterated it." The tune is popular around Galax as well, but there are striking differences in both style and melody from Tommy's version.

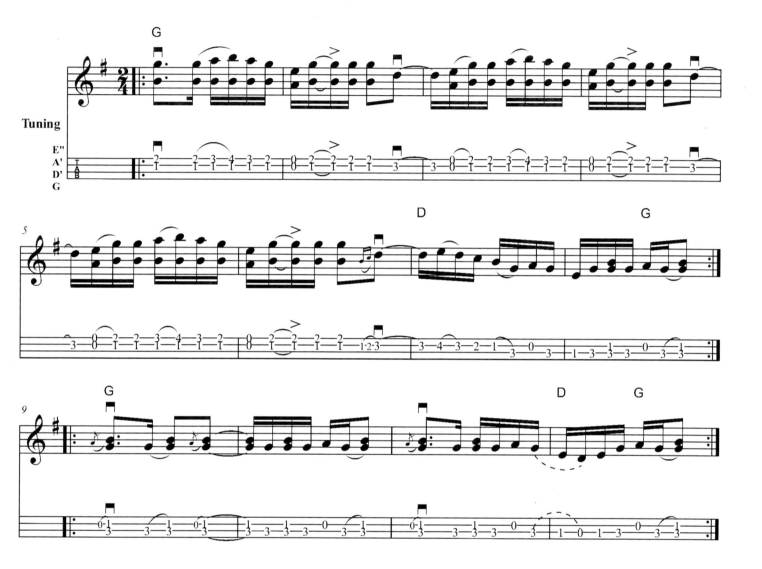

82. Sail Away Ladies

This haunting melody bears little resemblance to the tune that usually goes by this name. Tommy liked to tell the story of how he learned it from Pet McKinney: "He was an old Confederate veteran. I'd started to a dance when I was about 15 years old, and I had my fiddle under my arm when I met him in the road. He said 'Son, let me see your fiddle.' He took it and tuned it like this [GDAE]. That's the first time I ever heard a fiddle tuned that-a-way. He played that tune, and I said, 'How about playing it again, Mr. McKinney?' And he played it again for me. And I learned that tune right there." Tommy changed the tune a little bit, adding a phrase at the first ending of the high part.

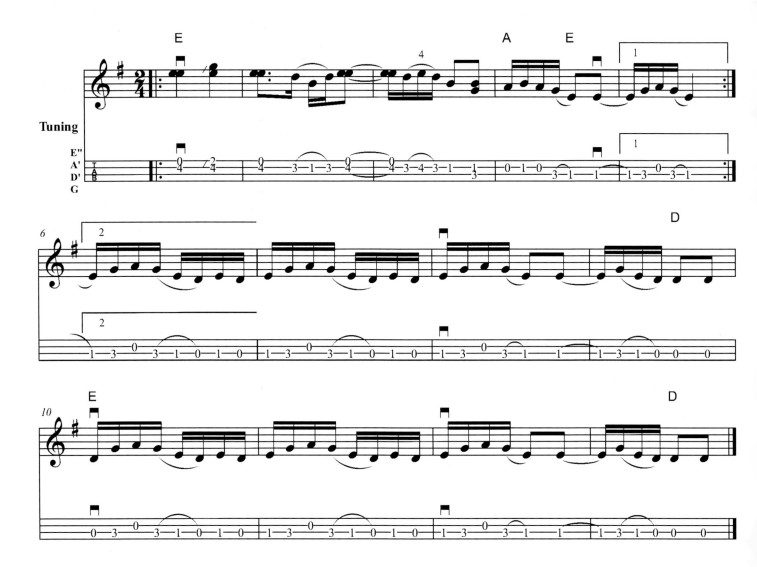

Sail away, sail away
Sail away ladies, sail away

83. Walking in My Sleep

Popularized by Arthur Smith on WSM's Grand Ole Opry radio broadcasts, this tune appears to be of relatively recent vintage but was learned by many of the older fiddlers in Surry, Grayson, and Carroll counties. Around Mount Airy, Pate Martin (1897-1963) was known for playing the tune, and Tommy learned it from him in the late 1920s or early '30s.

When you see that gal of mine, just tell her if you can
When she goes to make up bread, to wash them dirty hands

Chorus:
Walking in my sleep, babe, I'm walking in my sleep
Up and down that Dixie line, just walking in my sleep

When you see that gal of mine, tell her if you please
When she goes to make up dough, to roll them dirty sleeves

Pain in my finger, there's a pain in my toe
Pain in my anklebone, I ain't gonna work no more

Recommended listening, viewing, and reading

Recordings

American Fiddle Tunes, Rounder CD1518. One cut of John Rector playing "Old Dad."

Da Costa Woltz's Southern Broadcasters 1927-1929, Document CD-8023. Ben Jarrell, Tommy's father, on fiddle, with two banjos and a ukulele in various configurations.

Down to the Cider Mill, County Records CD-2734. Tommy Jarrell fiddling, solo and with banjo.

Joke on the Puppy, Mountain Records 310 (LP). Tommy fiddling, with banjo and guitar.

June Apple, Heritage Records HRC CD 038. Tommy fiddling, with banjo, fiddle, guitar, and bass.

The Legacy of Tommy Jarrell, vol. 1: Sail Away Ladies, County Records CD-2724. Tommy fiddling solo on some of his older and more unusual tunes. Liner notes by Barry Poss are especially informative.

The Legacy of Tommy Jarrell, vol. 2: Rainbow Sign, County Records CD-2725. Tommy fiddling, with banjo, mandolin and guitar.

The Legacy of Tommy Jarrell, vol. 4: Pickin' on Tommy's Porch, County Records CD-2727. Tommy fiddling, with banjo and guitar. Good liner notes by Mike Seeger.

Round Peak, vol. 1 and vol. 2, Field Recorders' Collective FRC109 and FRC110. Tommy (fiddle and banjo) and other Round Peak musicians in various combinations.

Sidna & Fulton Myers, Field Recorders' Collective FRC504. These musicians from Carroll County, Va., play on banjo and fiddle in an old style very much like Tommy Jarrell's. Born respectively in 1890 and 1894, they knew Tommy and, like him, learned some tunes from Logan Lowe.

Stay All Night and Don't Go Home, County Records CD-2735. Tommy fiddling, solo and with banjo.

Tommy & Fred, County Records CD-2702. Great recording of classic Round Peak fiddle-banjo duets, Tommy fiddling and Fred Cockerham on banjo.

Tommy Jarrell, vol. 1 and vol. 2, Field Recorders' Collective FRC211 and FRC212. Tommy fiddling in 1984 at the Country Dance and Song Society's Pinewoods Camp, with Paul Brown on banjo and Mike Seeger on guitar.

Video

A Visit with Tommy Jarrell: Solo Fiddle and Stories. Heath Curdts produced this limited-edition three-video series from home footage made during visits by Steve Barasch.

Bowing Lights, Southern Folklife Collection, University of North Carolina at Chapel Hill. Nancy Dols Neithammer, working in conjunction with Surry Community College, made this brilliant video of Tommy playing fiddle tunes in a dark room with a light attached to his wrist to document his bowing technique. You can get a copy from the Southern Folklife Collection for a nominal fee.

Jam at Low Gap School, Southern Folklife Collection, University of North Carolina–Chapel Hill. Another video of Tommy by Nancy Dols Neithammer, also available from the Southern Folklife Collection.

Legends of Old Time Music, Vestapol 3026DVD. Includes Tommy playing several tunes, as well as footage of other notables of old-time music.

Shady Grove: Old Time Music from North Carolina, Kentucky & Virginia, Vestapol 13071DVD. Tommy plays quite a few tunes on this anthology.

Sprout Wings and Fly and *My Old Fiddle: A Visit with Tommy Jarrell in the Blue Ridge,* Flower Films. Two documentaries on Tommy's music and stories from filmmaker Les Blank. The second video is a shorter follow-up to the first.

Printed sources

"Music from Round Peak," by Ray Alden. *Sing Out!* vol. 21, no. 6.

Strings of Life – Conversations with Old-Time Musicians from Virginia and North Carolina, by Kevin Donleavy, Pocahontas Press, Inc., Blacksburg, Va., 2004.

Liner notes to County CD-2702, *Tommy & Fred,* by Ray Alden.

Liner notes to County CD-2724, *The Legacy of Tommy Jarrell: Sail Away Ladies,* by Barry Poss.

"Tommy Jarrell's Family Stories, 1830-1925," parts I and II, by Nancy Dols Neithammer, *The Old-Time Herald* vol. 3, nos. 1 and 2.

Online

Digital Library of Appalachia, http://www.aca-dla.org. Many recordings of Tommy Jarrell's tunes and stories are archived here, most of them from a visit made by Wayne Erbsen and Andy Cahan in 1980.

Brad Letwich

Round Peak, 1998

Index of tunes

Index of musician profiles

courtesy David Lynch

Tommy Jarrell and Lily Scott, about 1917

About Brad Leftwich

Brad and Linda in 1984, back in the days when they were visiting Tommy Jarrell

Brad Leftwich was raised in Oklahoma, born into a family of old-time musicians who came to Kansas from Fancy Gap, Virginia, about 1907. His grandfather Rush Leftwich played clawhammer banjo; his great-uncle George Leftwich, fiddle; and his father, Dick, old-time guitar. Brad first learned guitar from his father and later took up the banjo and fiddle as a teenager. In 1973, he met the legendary Tommy Jarrell. Discovering a family connection created a strong bond between them, which, coupled with Tommy's charisma and musicianship, led Brad to devote many years to learning Tommy's style. Brad also visited and learned from other older musicians in Virginia, North Carolina, West Virginia, the Ozarks and Oklahoma.

Brad has been performing and recording since the mid-1970s. He began teaching fiddle in the 1980s and was one of the first "younger" old-time musicians to stress the importance of traditional bowing rhythms. Over the years he has developed a variety of techniques for passing on the tradition to new players. His skill as a fiddler is undisputed, and he easily ranks among the top old-time musicians of his generation. Brad now lives in Bloomington, Indiana, with his wife Linda Higginbotham, where they play with the Hogwire Stringband. Visit www.bradleftwich.net for more information about Brad's music.

Performing at the 2007 Swannanoa Gathering